What You Need To Know
TO SHOW
YOUR DOG

What You Need To Know TO SHOW YOUR DOG

Jeannie Burt

WYNWOOD™ Press
New York, New York

Library of Congress Cataloging-in-Publication Data

Burt, Jeannie.
    What you need to know to show your dog / Jeannie Burt:
illustrations by Linda Escher.
        p. cm.
    Includes bibliographical references.
    ISBN 0-922066-20-5 : $8.95
    1. Dogs—Showing. 2. Dog breeds. I. Title.
SF425.B87   1989
636.7'0888—dc20   89-16706
                                                        CIP

Copyright © 1989 by Jeannie Burt
Published by WYNWOOD™ Press
New York, New York
Printed in the United States of America

Contents

INTRODUCTION

At the time of this writing, there are 130 breeds* of dogs listed with the American Kennel Club. Each breed has its physical standards, its behavioral characteristics, and its idiosyncrasies. This guide can help you not only in selecting and purchasing a winning dog but also in determining whether the dog you already own is of show quality. And it can be a reliable resource the next time you're at a show and are wondering why some animals are winning ribbons and others are not!

On a more pragmatic level, this book can help you select a dog that is truly worth the higher price you may have to pay for it, and the valuable pricing guidelines will also help you be aware of a seller's overpricing.

Many people have asked me what dog is an overall "best" choice. There probably isn't one. Everyone's taste is his own. For quite a while the Cocker Spaniel has been the most popular dog in the United States. Small wonder—it is beautiful and is a wonderful family dog that can be happy running in the

---

* This number includes *both* varieties of the Fox Terrier breed—the Smooth Fox Terrier and the Wirehaired Fox Terrier

country or at home in a city apartment. There are, however, breeds reviewed here that are rare but that might be *your* best choice. I would advise you to sit down alone or with any prospective co-owners and do some planning before you decide on a particular dog. Think hard about:

• *How much exercise you can give the animal, and how much it needs*. Most breeds that have been developed for hard work or sport need a daily workout outside. Others, Toys especially, are normally content and healthy inside a small apartment.

• *How much time you want to spend grooming your dog*. Most long- and wirehaired breeds require attentive grooming; short-haired breeds need less time. Some owners have considerable time to spend grooming their animals, and look forward to it; others do not. Also, depending on the breed, some grooming standards for show are rigorous; others require simply that the dog be clean.

• *The size of animal you want*. These are guidelines only as each of the terms is relative; what seems small to some will seem larger to others. The Toys normally weigh ten pounds or less; the small dogs weigh about ten to twenty-five pounds. Medium-sized dogs are normally between twenty-six and seventy pounds; the large dogs range from seventy-one to ninety pounds, and the giants weigh ninety pounds and more (sometimes a lot more).

• *Whether you want an animal to be active or docile, or somewhere in between*. Some dogs that do not need lots of outdoor exercise are still very active indoors.

• *How fastidious you are*. There are breeds that are as clean as cats, and there are others with long, thick coats that may shed not once but twice a year. Be fair to yourself as well as to your dog.

Once you have decided on the breed you want, how do you go about finding one that meets your standards?

Most important, do not go to the nearest pet shop. Pups there are precious to look at but often are sickly and have no criteria for breeding. As you read further, you will note that some breeds are particularly vulnerable to the pet shop/puppy mill breeders' fads. It is best to stay away from them.

To find a healthy animal, go to a reputable breeder. You can find one through word of mouth or from reliable resources like your veterinarian, the Dog Fanciers' association, *Pure-Bred Dogs/American Kennel Gazette*, and *Dog Fancy* magazine (the July issue gives a listing of the clubs that specialize in AKC breeds).

For each of the 130 AKC breeds, I have included a general description as well as an idea of the care and grooming you should expect to give. Moderate grooming indicates weekly or semiweekly attention; heavy grooming indicates attention almost daily. Trimming means clipping or scissor cutting—your breeder can show you how to trim your particular animal. Stripping is a part of grooming that requires dead hairs to be removed or plucked (most wirehaired breeds require it). Ask your breeder for help, or learn from a professional groomer.

Additional categories for each breed cover the following:

coat: Here you will find a description of the breed's coat type and the colors that are acceptable for show.

height/weight: These are averages, but most competitions require show animals to be very close to the standards listed if not exactly within them. Where a height or a weight is not given, there is no standard given for that category. (A dog's height is measured from ground to withers—the top part of the shoulders just behind the neck.)

behavior: Each breed has its own personality and energy level. Here you will find those qualities of behavior that are typical of the breed. Obviously you can find individual animals that do not behave as outlined, but the guidelines will indicate the tendencies of each breed. Look here also for a description of the needs of each breed for exercise and companionship. Moderate exercise indicates a daily walk for half an hour or so; lots of exercise means just that—lots—daily running for an hour or more and space to run outside throughout the day.

winning traits: Here you will find the basic traits that make a champion in each breed. There is a description of each significant aspect of the dog and the traits judges will look for in a winner.

disqualify/penalize: Listed in this category are those traits that will count against a breed or possibly disqualify it completely from the ring. What may penalize an animal of one breed may not penalize one of another breed. These standards are breed-specific.

considerations: Here are listed general health problems and items of particular interest in each breed. As a general rule, hip dysplasia is a problem in the larger breeds, sensitivity to climate is found most often in the shorthaired breeds, and fragility is most common to the Toys.

price range: This is the price you are likely to pay for a show-quality pup. You can find less expensive dogs that will make wonderful pets. Prices also vary depending on your geographical area and whether the dog you have chosen is currently in vogue. When price ranges are too broad, you will find the minimum price you should expect to pay for a show-quality animal; an upper-end price will not be listed.

There are seven standard breed classifications:

Herding
Hound
Nonsporting
Sporting
Terrier
Toy
Working

The *Herding* dogs were developed for herding and protecting. The larger Herding breeds (Belgian Malinois, Belgian Sheepdog, Belgian Tervuren, Bouvier des Flandres; Briard, Collie, German Shepherd, Old English Sheepdog) are strong and vocal and "will" their flocks by their outstanding size. The smaller breeds (Australian Cattle Dog, Bearded Collie, Puli, Shetland Sheepdog, Cardigan Welsh Corgi and the Pembroke Welsh Corgi) are faster and nip at heels to move their herds or keep animals in line. Because their nature is to protect, all the Herding group should be acquired when they are quite young to promote good relations with people. They also should be exercised and let outside often because they are naturally active.

The *Hounds* are broken into three subgroups: hounds developed to hunt by scent (American Foxhound, Basset, Beagle, Black and Tan Coonhound, Bloodhound, English Foxhound, and Harrier); those that hunt by sight (Afghan, Borzoi, Greyhound, Ibizan, Irish Wolfhound, Pharaoh Hound, Saluki, Scottish Deerhound, and Whippet); and hounds that are a combination of both sight and scent (Basenji, Dachshund, Norwegian Elkhound, Otter Hound, and Rhodesian Ridgeback). As a group they make wonderful pets and fit gracefully into most families. The larger of these animals, however, need hours of running and exercise daily.

The *Nonsporting* group is really a catchall for breeds that do not fit into other categories. They are the most diverse of any group and have not been developed with any special purpose in mind. Within this group are the Bichon Frise, Boston Terrier, Bulldog, Chow Chow, Dalmatian, Finnish Spitz, French Bulldog, Keeshond, Lhasa Apso, Poodle (miniature and standard), Schipperke, Tibetan Spaniel, and Tibetan Terrier.

The *Sporting* dogs are those that were developed specifically to hunt. They are segregated into groups with particular talents. The *pointers* (Pointer is also a breed) are the German Shorthaired and German Wirehaired, the Vizsla, Weimaraner, and Wirehaired Pointing Griffon. The *setters*, namely the English, Gordon, and Irish setters, all find game and show it to the hunter either by pointing at it or by sinking to the ground with their bodies directed toward it. The *retriever* group comprises the Chesapeake Bay, Curly-Coated, Flat-Coated, Golden, and Labrador retrievers, who all stay with their hunters and bring back the game from water or land. The *spaniels* are the American Water, Brittany, Clumber, Cocker, English Cocker, English Springer, Field, Irish Water, Sussex, and Welsh Springer; they are the dogs that flush the game. As a group, the Sporting dogs need plenty of room to run in order to be happy and healthy, and are best kept in an area where they can be outside and active.

The *Terriers* are perhaps the most delightful handfuls of all. Originally they were bred to help keep down populations of burrowing vermin. They were the dogs not of aristocrats but of the working people, and as a whole the Terriers are spunky and fun-loving. They are the Airedale, American Staffordshire, Australian, Bedlington, Border, Bull, Cairn, Dandie Dinmont, Fox (both smooth and wirehaired), Irish, Kerry Blue, Lakeland, Manchester (standard), Miniature Schnauzer, Norfolk, Norwich, Scottish, Sealyham, Skye, Soft-Coated Wheaten, Staffordshire Bull, Welsh, and the West Highland White. As a group, however, all but the smooth-coated demand more attentive care in grooming than most of the other breeds.

Toys are the smallest of the dog breeds. Although they can guard by alerting the family to intruders, and occasionally they hunt, they were developed purely for the enjoyment of their companionship. The group is a mixture of shorthaired dogs (the shorthaired Brussels Griffon, shorthaired Chihuahua, Italian Greyhound, Toy Manchester Terrier, Miniature Pinscher, Pug); wirehaired dogs (Affenpinscher and wirehaired Brussels Griffon); and long-haired dogs (the long-haired Chihuahua, English Toy Spaniel, Japanese Chin, Maltese, Papillon, Pekingese, Pomeranian, Toy Poodle, Shih Tzu, Silky Terrier, and Yorkshire Terrier). Because of their size and talent for companionship, the Toys make the most splendid pets when space is limited and the need for companionship is great.

The *Working* dogs are normally large and energetic and because of their size and intelligence are truly dogs that were developed to work. Their acumen for duty can be broken into three categories: sledding, guarding, and rescuing. *Sledding dogs* (Alaskan Malamute, Samoyed, and Siberian Husky) were bred to thrive in the bitterest wind and temperatures. *Guarding dogs* (Akita, Bernese Mountain Dog, Boxer, Bullmastiff, Doberman Pinscher, Giant Schnauzer, Great Dane, Great Pyrenees, Komondor, Kuvasz, Mastiff, Rottweiler, and Standard Schnauzer) are excellent protectors, whether over flocks or humans. *Rescuers* (Newfoundland, Portuguese Water Dog, and Saint Bernard) are noted for their courage in rescuing victims in water or on land. As a whole, the Working dog needs lots of space to run and work in order to maintain health and happiness.

Only you know what you want in a dog—from a companion

that quietly waits for your attention, to a big, rambunctious fellow. Your success with your dog in the show ring will depend on your rapport with him, his conformity to the standards for his breed, and your care and grooming with him before showtime.

This book was written with love and respect for dogs. I hope that you find it enjoyable, and that with its help you can find your ideal dog. Choose well, and perhaps both of you will become champions!

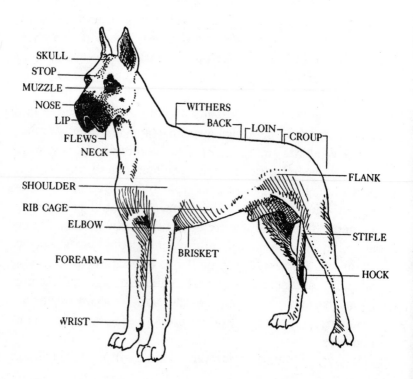

AFFENPINSCHER (Toy)

Also known as the monkey dog for his bushy eyebrows, mustache, and staring eyes, this little dog may be small but is not at all delicate. He has a small, apple head and a short, pointed nose, and he makes an excellent pet and companion. Expect some grooming and trimming.

coat: Depending on parts of body is short, shaggy, thick, and stiff, wiry on legs and face. *Colors:* black, black with tan, red, gray.

height/weight: Not more than 10¼″ at shoulder/approx. 7 lbs.

behavior: A very quick learner, gentle, fun-loving, and likes everyone. May bark more than other breeds, is lively, demanding, can be nervous and somewhat shy, and normally too high-strung for children. High activity level even indoors, does not need much outdoor exercise.

winning traits: Overall, a small, sturdy animal with a scraggy coat; *head* round with a domed forehead and skull, short muzzle and a lower jaw that is longer than the upper jaw; *ears* clipped, pointed, small and high-set; *legs* are as straight as possible when seen from front and back; *body* has a straight back, moderately deep brisket, and a loin that is somewhat tucked up; tail is docked and carried high.

disqualify/penalize: Colors that are too light, white markings, teeth that show, animals that are over the size standard, ears that are not erect, eyes that are not black.

considerations: Suffers easily from broken bones, prone to slipped stifle (knee), may have breathing difficulties and minor skin problems.

price range: Over $200.

AFGHAN HOUND (Hound)

Discovered in Afghanistan in the nineteenth century, this breed hunts by sight and is sufficiently swift and agile for deer, gazelles, and hare. Normally aloof and elegant, the Afghan makes a lovely, quiet companion. Expect a lot of grooming and heavy shedding.

coat: Long, thick, silky, and fine everywhere but along the top of the back, where it is short. *Colors:* any color permissible.

height/weight: Dog 27″/60 lbs., bitch 25″/50 lbs.

behavior: Can be a slow learner, is a one-family dog, gentle with everyone but can be aloof even with owner. Potential for nervousness in some animals, needs patience while training. Though inactive indoors, needs lots of outdoor exercise.

winning traits: Overall is aristocratic, graceful and proud; *head* is long and refined with a definite topknot of long hair and long strong jaws; *ears* are long and silky and begin about eye level; *neck* is arched; *legs*, front are long, straight and strong, hind legs long and bent at the stifle for speed; *body* has a straight, level back with a strong loin and high, pronounced hips; *tail* is curled out and up with less hair than the rest of the body.

disqualify/penalize: Over/undershot jaw, absence of top-

knot, muzzle that is too short, white markings, eyes that are light-colored, round or bulgy, neck that is too short or thick or curved wrong (like a goose's), humped back or swayback, hips that are not prominent, brisket that is too wide, tail that is too bushy, carried over back, or carried sideways, legs that swing in or out when moving, feet that are too small, excessive shyness.
considerations: May develop hip dysplasia, cataracts, tends to react to medication badly.
price range: $250–$450.

AIREDALE (Terrier)

This fellow's extreme agility and keen eyesight make him an outstanding hunter, but he is also used as a guard and as a guide dog for the blind. He is the largest of the Terriers. There is a dignity and confidence about him that adds to his good looks. Needs attentive grooming, stripping, and trimming with a professional hand. Sheds little.

coat: Wiry, thick. *Colors:* head and ears tan, body black, white spot on chest permissible.
height/weight: Approx. 23"/50 lbs.
behavior: A very intelligent, quick learner. Friendly with everyone, but a good guard dog. Adaptable, rowdy when young, fun-loving. Very active even indoors, may be too active for young children, needs a lot of outdoor exercise.

winning traits: Overall a leggy, rugged animal that has a bright alert carriage; *head* is long and flat and moderately wide; *ears* are V-shaped and set toward the side of the head; *legs,* front are very straight and well muscled with a moderately heavy bone, hind legs are long with powerful thighs that are parallel when seen from behind; *body* has a short, straight back with wide muscular loins; *tail* is docked fairly long and is carried high but not over back.

disqualify/penalize: Poor movement (not free) or movement with toes that point in or out, yellow eyes, over/undershot jaw, white feet, coat that is too soft, ears like a hound's, tail that curls or droops.

considerations: May develop hip dysplasia, may be prone to skin allergies.

price range: $250–$400.

AKITA (Working)

This breed, a national monument in Japan, is the symbol of happiness and good health. It was brought to the United States by occupation soldiers in World War II and is increasing in popularity. They make wonderful hunters, guard dogs, and gentle, proud friends. Expect moderate grooming and shedding.

coat: Double, straight, full, short, harsh. *Colors:* any that are distinct and clear.

height/weight: Dog 26″–28″, bitch 24″–26″.

behavior: A quick learner, mild-mannered with everyone but intruders. Loves his family, including children, may be aloof with strangers, can be very single-minded and stubborn, is very faithful. Needs lots of outdoor exercise.

winning traits: Overall is a powerful and heavy animal that has a very active and intelligent bearing; *head* is very large and broad but not out of balance with body, muzzle is broad and strong; *ears* are small and very erect, wide at root and rounded at tip; *legs,* front are strong, heavily boned, and set back on shoulders, hindquarters have very well muscled thighs and are straight when seen from behind; *tail* is long and curled up over the back.

disqualify/penalize: Any kind of feathering or ruff, bent or drop ears, a nose that is pink or without pigmentation in any but the white dogs, ears that are not erect.

considerations: May develop hip dysplasia, is prone to hypothyroidism and skin allergies.

price range: $300–$450.

ALASKAN MALAMUTE
(Working)

Named after the native Mahl-emuts tribe, this one is a grand sled dog. He is well muscled, powerful, heavy-boned, and has the ability to adapt to all climates and conditions. He makes a superior working dog. Expect a lot of shedding and moderate grooming.

coat: Thick, coarse, with a heavy, dense undercoat. *Colors:* gray like wolves', black and white, all white.

height/weight: Dog 25"/85 lbs., bitch 23"/75 lbs.

behavior: May learn slowly, requiring patient training coupled with very little indulgence. Is friends with everyone, very good with children but may be too playful for some. May howl a lot, males may fight with other dogs. Needs lots of outdoor exercise, may not do well in apartment living.

winning traits: Overall a very strong, compact dog with great endurance and intelligent bearing; *head* is broad and strong with a furrow between the eyes and a very large muzzle; *ears* are somewhat small, erect, set wide on the head with the lowest point in line with the eyes; *legs* are heavily boned, very strong, and widely placed both front and back; *body* is compact and short with a strong, straight back and strong loins; *tail* is carried in a curl over the back.

disqualify/penalize: Blue eyes, unsound or weak legs or feet, weak back, gait that is stilted or not strong, lightness of bone, high-set ears, tail that curls too tightly and rests on back.

considerations: May develop hip dysplasia, breed prone to dwarfism and skin problems due to zinc deficiencies.
price range: $200 and up.

AMERICAN FOXHOUND
(Hound)

Friend and companion to George Washington, this is the ultimate hunting dog. He is trainable to any ground game, and can be used for field trials, as a trail hound, in hunting with guns, or for hunting in packs. He has a good voice and the endurance to hunt all day. Expect moderate grooming and shedding.

coat: Shiny, close, hard. *Colors:* any.
height/weight: Dog 22″–25″, bitch 21″–24″/60 lbs.
behavior: May learn slowly, loves everyone including children, does not like to be alone. Can be strong-willed but mild-mannered, may roam, tends to bay excessively. Needs lots of outdoor exercise.
winning traits: Overall a strong, eager animal with strong, free movement; *head* is long and wide with a straight, square-cut muzzle; *ears* are long, set low, and are not erect; *legs*, front are straight and somewhat heavily boned, hind are straight when viewed from behind and muscular; *body* is strong and long with wide loins that are somewhat arched; *tail* is natural and carried up and high (not over back).

disqualify/penalize: High-set ears, nose that turns up or is Roman, short neck, sway or hump back, chest that is too wide, crooked legs, too little muscle in hindquarters, cowhocks or hocks that are too straight, tail that is too long, curving like a teapot, carried forward, or without a brush, coat that is too short or soft.

considerations: Genetically one of the healthiest dogs but can develop hip dysplasia and deafness.

price range: $150–$250.

AMERICAN STAFFORDSHIRE TERRIER
(Terrier)

Contrary to its name, the breed originated in England from a cross of the Bulldog and the Terrier. He is used now as a guard dog, but at one time was used for fighting. He gives the impression of strength and confidence. Needs moderate grooming, sheds moderately.

coat: Short, stiff, smooth, shiny. *Colors:* any.

height/weight: Dog 18″–19″, bitch 17″–18″.

behavior: A quick learner, good with everyone, including children, if his family is around, but if his family is not present he may terrorize others. May attack other dogs. Needs inordinate amounts of exercise.

winning traits: Overall, an animal of immense strength for its size and one that is agile and intelligent; *head* is very broad and has high cheeks, moderately long with a deep muzzle and jaws that are very strong; *ears* are either uncropped or cropped, if uncropped they should prick or droop slightly at the top; *legs*, front are large-boned, straight, and wide-set on shoulders, hind are powerful and straight when seen from behind; *body* has a wide, deep brisket, short, straight back that has a slight slope up from tail; *tail* is natural, short-set, low, and tapering.

disqualify/penalize: Eyes that are light-colored or pink light or pink, tail long or badly carried, under/overshot jaw, pink nose, coat that is more than 80 percent white.

considerations: Normally healthy but may develop hip dysplasia.

price range: $150–$300.

AMERICAN WATER SPANIEL (Sporting)

This breed makes a wonderful gun dog and retriever. Instead of pointing game, he springs it. When retrieving in water, he will use his tail as a rudder. The breed is one of only a small number of dogs native to the United States. Expect moderate grooming and shedding.

coat: Tight curls, thick enough to protect in the water and in difficult ground cover. *Colors:* liver or dark chocolate, small amount of white on toes or chest permissible.

height/weight: 15"–18"/dog 28–45 lbs., bitch 25–40 lbs.

behavior: A quick learner, may become attached to one person but is friendly with everyone; may not be patient with rough children. Lively, may drool, bark, or whine more than most. Can be active indoors, needs a lot of outdoor exercise.

winning traits: Overall a strong, durable, medium-sized dog; *head* is somewhat broad and long with a square, medium-length muzzle and a proud carriage; *ears* hang and are long and wide, beginning just above the line of the eyes; *legs*, front are medium-long, fairly straight and strong, hind are strong with bent stifles for good movement; *body* is strong with a deep chest and strong loins; *tail* is slightly curved and normally carried a little lower than the line of the back.

disqualify/penalize: Flat or narrow skull, muzzle that is slender or too long, rat tail, shaved tail, coat too straight, soft, fine, or too kinked, yellow eyes, cowhocks.

considerations: May be prone to losing patches of hair.

price range: $250 and up.

AUSTRALIAN CATTLE DOG (Herding)

These small dogs are capable of working herds in the vast areas of Australia. They have a quiet, alert stamina and control the wildest herds by biting at the cattle's heels rather than barking and startling the animals. Expect minimal grooming and moderate shedding.

coat: Short, coarse, thick. *Colors:* blue (solid or mottled blue, with or without markings of black, darker blue, or tan, with tan on legs and shorter tan undercoat), or red speckle (reddish specks all over, some with darker red markings on head); pups are born white, turning later to adult colors.

height/weight: Dog 18″–20″, bitch 17″–19″.

behavior: A quick learner, is very good with his family, can be overly suspicious with strangers. Extremely alert and active, easily trained. Needs lots of outdoor exercise.

winning traits: Overall a very strong, sturdy animal with power and stamina as well as agility; *head* is wide with a light curve between the ears, a broad forehead and a moderately long, powerful, and deep muzzle; *ears* are long and wide and start just above the line of the eye; *legs* are wide-set, strong-boned, and straight when seen from front and behind; *body* has a straight, strong back with a deep, strong chest, deep flanks, and a wide loin; *tail* is natural and low-set.

disqualify/penalize: Black markings on body, straight shoulders, stilted or weak movement, cowhocks, over/undershot jaw, tail carried above back line at any time, animals that

are over or under the size mentioned above, tail without hair.
considerations: May develop hip dysplasia and be prone to
deafness.
price range: $200–$300.

AUSTRALIAN TERRIER
(Terrier)

Five kinds of British Terriers
were the forerunners of this
breed. It has the liveliness and
assurance typical of the Terrier
but may be easier to train than
most other Terriers. It has
good speed to hunt rabbits
and rats but is now used mainly
as a companion and house
pet. Expect moderate grooming, stripping, and trimming,
which can be done by the non-
professional. Sheds little.

coat: Rough, straight. *Colors:* bluish black or silver black with
tan (the richer colors are most desirable), or sandy red on the
head and legs.
height/weight: 10″/12–14 lbs.
behavior: A quick learner, loves its family but can be aloof
with strangers. Wants to please, lively and alert, likes children
if they are not rough. Good for almost any environment, including apartment.

winning traits: Overall a small, spirited animal with a balanced appearance and a harsh coat; *head* long and flat with a topknot; *ears* are small, high-set, and prick; *legs*, front are straight and sturdy, hind are muscled with medium bones and small feet; *body* is somewhat long and low with a chest that is medium-wide and deep; *tail* is docked and carried high but not gaily or over back.

disqualify/penalize: Protruding or light-colored eyes, nose that is flesh-colored, over/undershot mouth, white on chest or feet.

considerations: None.

price range: $250 and up.

BASENJI (Hound)

While this breed is known as the barkless dog, they do have a sound somewhat like a yodel. They make excellent hunters and can be trained to retrieve game, point, and track injured animals. They are as clean and fastidious as cats. Need little grooming and shed little.

coat: Silky and short. *Colors:* chestnut (deepest colors best), black, or black and tan with white feet, chest and tip of tail.

height/weight: Dog 17"/24 lbs., bitch 16"/22 lbs.

behavior: A very quick learner, can be quarrelsome with strange dogs. Most love their families but some are reticent in forming human attachments. Extremely lively, very active in or out of doors, needs fair amount of outdoor exercise.

winning traits: Overall a proud, intense animal with alert and intelligent bearing; *head* has a flat skull, a round, tidy muzzle, and a wrinkled forehead; *ears* are prick, small, and high-set on head; *legs*, front are straight and fine, hind are strong and straight from behind; *body* has a short, straight back, deep chest, and a strong loin; *tail* is carried in a tight curl over back.

disqualify/penalize: Low-set or droopy ears, head that is domed or peaked, round eyes, over/undershot mouth, wide chest, wide hindquarters, heavy bone, cream-colored coat, or colors not mentioned above.

considerations: Normally healthy but can be prone to genetic hemloytic anemia and allergies.

price range: $200–$300.

BASSET HOUND (Hound)

The breed originated in France, where it was developed to follow small game through very difficult terrain. Though they may be slow, they are brave and tenacious and have an exceptional nose for the hunt. Some hunters say that their sound when "giving tongue" is the most beautiful of all of the dogs. Expect moderate grooming.

coat: Hard and short. *Colors:* any hound colors with any markings.

height/weight: 11"–15"/40–60 lbs.

behavior: A somewhat slow learner, good with everyone including children. May be hard to housebreak, placid, gentle. Will fit into city living but is basically an outside dog needing outside exercise.

winning traits: Overall a short, heavy animal with a methodical, even temperament; *head* is large, domed, and medium-wide with loose, wrinkled skin, hanging muzzle; *ears* are extremely long, set low and very far back on the head; *legs*, front are short, heavy-boned, and straight when seen from front, hind are short, heavy, very well muscled, and are straight when seen from behind.

disqualify/penalize: Over/undershot jaw, cowhocks or bowed legs, coat that is too long, front legs that knuckle over, height above that mentioned above.

considerations: Ears may get in the animal's way and become injured, is normally healthy but can easily become lame or have back problems, may develop glaucoma and digestive problems. **price range:** $200–$300.

BEAGLE (Hound)

This is the favorite Hound in the United States and Canada, an excellent gun dog for small ground game and pheasants. He is also one of the most popular house dogs. His bay may sound sad to someone not familiar with the breed, but to those who know him it usually is a sound of joy. Needs moderate grooming.

coat: Hard, close, medium length. *Colors:* any hound color, usually white with variations of tan or tan and black.
height/weight: Two classes—under 13″/approx. 18 lbs.; 13″–15″/approx. 20 lbs.
behavior: A quick learner, affectionate, tolerant, gentle with and likes everyone, including children. Gets along well with strange dogs, needs firm, patient training, may bay a lot. Is active indoors and out, needs some outside exercise.
winning traits: Overall a clean, alert animal with a short-coupled, tidy body; *head* is somewhat long and wide with medium-length square muzzle; *ears* are hanging, velvety, rounded at bottom edge, and turned slightly toward the cheek; *legs*, front are straight and well-boned, hind are strong and

straight when seen from behind, with moderately-bent stifle; *body* is short, strong, and has a proud neck and carriage; *tail* is natural, carried high, and has a slight curve.

disqualify/penalize: Head that is too flat or too domed, muzzle that is too short, too long, or snipy, ears that are too short or set too high, neck that is short or thick, chest that is too wide or not deep enough, back that is too long, sway or roach, crooked legs, tail that is too long, has a teapot curve, or has no brush, coat that is too short or too thin, animal that measures over 15".

considerations: Normally healthy but may have heart problems, epilepsy, and back problems.

price range: $200–$250.

BEARDED COLLIE (Herding)

Though the Beardies were painted by Gainsborough in 1717, it was not until 1969 that the Bearded Collie Club of America was formed. The breed, developed in England, makes a superior herding and droving dog, but is still one of the rarer breeds in the United States. Expect moderate to heavy grooming and shedding.

coat: Double outercoat is straight or slightly wavy, shaggy, and natural (left untrimmed even for show). *Colors:* black, gray, brown, red fawn with white markings on the face and before the shoulders. Pups are black, brown, blue, or fawn, and may not have the markings that develop later.

height/weight: Dog 21"–22", bitch 20"–21".

behavior: A quick learner, loves everyone, including active children. Mild-mannered, gentle. Needs lots of outdoor exercise.

winning traits: Overall a very strong, medium-sized dog with a long and somewhat slender body and a quizzical expression; *head* is wide, flat, and has a strong muzzle; *ears* hang and are set level with eyes; *legs,* front are well-boned and straight, hind are muscular with low hocks and are straight when seen from behind; *body* is long and has a straight back that makes a gentle curve to the rump, the chest is deep and the loin strong; *tail* is natural, medium-long, and low-set with a slight curve.

disqualify/penalize: Coat that is too long or an animal that is trimmed, under/oversized animals, snipy muzzle, a lower back (croup) that is flat or steep.

considerations: Prone to hip dysplasia.

price range: $400 and up.

BEDLINGTON TERRIER
(Terrier)

The coal town of Bedlington, England, named this breed. The unusual silhouette with high, arched loins and deep chest mark him as special. In the eighteenth century the breed had short legs for ratting. Later, possibly by cross-breeding with the Whippet, it developed to its present line. Needs lots of grooming and trimming, probably from a professional groomer.

coat: Mixture of soft and hard hairs, thick, curly for show, must not exceed 1″ long on body but can be a little longer on legs. *Colors:* blue, sandy, liver, and tan.

height/weight: Dog 16½″, bitch 15½″/17–23 lbs.

behavior: A quick learner, normally a one-family dog, gets along with everyone including strangers, best with grown children. Lively (as are most Terriers), can be strong-willed. Active indoors and out, needs some outdoor exercise.

winning traits: Overall a very limber animal with graceful, lamblike appearance and arched back; *head* is slender but rounded, with a muzzle that is somewhat long and a short skull that has a woolly topknot; *ears* hang and are triangular in shape with a little tassle of hair at the tip; *legs* are long, strong, and lithe, back legs longer than front legs, the forelegs from front view forming a wedge that is widest at the shoulders.

disqualify/penalize: Tail carried over back or tightly to under-body, coat more than 1″ long, a weaving or paddle gait.
considerations: Normally healthy but may develop eye or liver problems.
price range: $350 and up.

BELGIAN MALINOIS
(Herding)

This breed is rare in the United States. They make outstanding sheepdogs and guard dogs. The silhouette is elegant and the carriage of the head proud, with a close resemblance to the German Shepherd. They need attentive grooming. Expect somewhat heavy shedding.

coat: Short, straight. *Colors:* rich fawn to mahogany, black face mask.
height/weight: Dog 22½″–27½″, bitch 20½″–25½″/approx. 60 lbs.
behavior: A very quick learner, active, intelligent, tends to be a one-family dog. Good with grown children, aloof with strangers. Needs lots of outdoor exercise.
winning traits: Overall a muscular, sturdy animal with a balanced square silhouette and regal carriage; *head* is strong and balanced with the rest of the body, and has a pointed, clean muzzle that is free of excess skin; *ears* are very erect, triangular, and the root is at eye level; *legs*, front are straight with oval-

shaped bone, hind legs are strong with muscular thighs, straight when seen from behind, with long feet; *body* has a straight, short back that slopes up slightly from the tail to the withers, and a deep chest; *tail* is natural, hangs with a slight curl when relaxed.

disqualify/penalize: Washed-out fawn color on body, hanging houndlike ears, cropped or stumpy tail, over or under size.

considerations: Normally healthy but may develop hip dysplasia.

price range: $200–$300.

BELGIAN SHEEPDOG
(Herding)

Another name for the breed is Groenendael. Very elegant, alert, and completely devoted to their masters, these protective sheepdogs make excellent guard dogs as well. During World War I thousands were used as messengers. Expect daily grooming and heavy shedding.

coat: Very thick, the outer coat being long, straight, and somewhat harsh. *Colors:* solid black, black with some white on chest, back toes, chin and muzzle.

height/weight: Dog 22½″–27½″, bitch 20½″–25½″/approx. 60 lbs.

behavior: An extremely quick learner, very good with children if introduced early in dog's life. Obedient, normal dogs are gentle with everyone, but can be reserved with strangers (abnormal animals of this breed may be vicious, timid, excitable, volatile—know your breeder well before selecting an animal from this breed). Needs lots of outdoor exercise.

winning traits: Overall a square-built dog with power, agility, and grace; *head* flat on top and strong with a pointed, moderately long muzzle; *ears* are triangular with the root at about eye level; *legs* straight, muscular, and parallel, with very well muscled thighs that give straight fluid movement; *body* has a straight, short, broad back and deep chest; *tail* natural and carried low when relaxed and in line with back when in motion.

disqualify/penalize: Ears that hang like those of the Hound, viciousness, tail that is stumpy or cropped, over/undersized animals, wiry or silky coat.

considerations: May develop hip dysplasia.

price range: $200–$300.

BELGIAN TERVUREN
(Herding)

This guarding and herding dog takes its name from a village in Belgium. But for color it is almost identical to the Belgian Sheepdog. For show purposes the male should appear distinctly masculine and the female distinctly feminine. Expect moderate to heavy shedding and daily grooming.

coat: Very thick with a long, straight outercoat. *Colors:* fawn to mahogany with a black mask and overlay.

height/weight: Dog 24"–26", bitch 22"–24"/approx. 60 lbs.

behavior: See *Belgian Sheepdog.*

winning traits: Overall an elegant medium-sized animal with a square, muscular profile; *head* is wedge-shaped and flat with a strong, somewhat pointed muzzle; *ears* are triangular, erect, and high-set; *legs* are oval-boned, muscular, and parallel, with wide-set, muscular thighs; *body* is moderately wide with a straight back and deep chest; *tail* is low when relaxed, and level with back when in movement or excited.

disqualify/penalize: Hanging ears, docked or stumpy tail, white except on chest, toes, chin or muzzle, all black or all liver-colored animals, undershot teeth, over/undersized animals.

considerations: Normally healthy but may develop hip dysplasia and can lose coloration in skin and hair.

price range: $200–$300.

BERNESE MOUNTAIN DOG
(Working)

These big dogs were bred for harness in Switzerland. They make wonderful guard dogs and watchdogs. The breed is rare in the United States, but has been known in its native land for almost two thousand years. Expect moderate grooming and shedding.

coat: Long, silky, wavy. *Colors:* must be symmetrical, black with russet or tan markings on legs, white markings on chest, just above forelegs, and on face.

height/weight: Dog 23"–27½", bitch 21"–26"/approx. 65 lbs.

behavior: A very quick learner, loves to be with its family, may be timid and aloof with strangers. Gentle, obedient, easygoing, wonderful with children. Needs lots of outdoor exercise.

winning traits: Overall a large, strong, and intelligent animal with strength and endurance for hard work; *head* is moderately wide and flat; *ears* hang and are medium in size with a rounded tip; *legs*, front are set somewhat back on shoulders and are straight and powerful, hind are wide, powerful, and straight when viewed from behind; *body* is square with a straight, wide back and deep, broad chest; *tail* is long (at least to the hocks), merry, and carried low when relaxed, in line with body when animated or in motion.

disqualify/penalize: Too large head, light eyes, too heavy or long ears, over/undershot mouth, curled tail, white legs, color other than mentioned above.

considerations: May be prone to hip dysplasia, bone disease, and digestive problems; may develop abnormalities in eyelids.
price range: $350–$450.

BICHON FRISE (Nonsporting)

These relatively small but sturdy animals love water and are descendants of the Water Spaniel. They began as pampered pets of the Italian and French nobility, but since World War II have become increasingly popular in the United States. Expect attentive grooming and trimming that requires professional ability. With proper maintenance, sheds little.

coat: Double, soft, thick, springy and puffy. *Colors:* white or having shades of apricot or cream (as long as the shading covers less than 10 percent of overall coloring).
height/weight: 9½″–11½″.
behavior: A quick learner, loves everyone, including lively children. Fairly easily trained but may be difficult to housebreak. Active indoors but does not need a great deal of outdoor exercise.
winning traits: Overall an animal that is moderately small with a sturdy build and a playful personality; *head* has a topknot that makes it look round and has a moderately short and strong

muzzle and jaw; *ears* hang, have long hair, and are set a little higher than eye level; *legs* are medium-boned with muscular thighs and are straight when seen from front or back; *body* has a straight back and a moderately wide chest; *tail* is natural and set high and curled over back.

disqualify/penalize: Wiry or silky coat, lack of undercoat, animals that are over 12″ or under 9″, back leg movement that is not straight when viewed from behind, cowhocks, a dog that is not cheerful and playful, corkscrew tail, yellow, blue, or gray eyes, eyes that are not ringed with black.

considerations: Prone to skin problems, low blood sugar, and cataracts.

price range: $350 and up.

BLACK AND TAN COONHOUND (Hound)

This fellow hunts solely by his nose, barking when he has treed his quarry. He is agile and powerful and is willing to hunt at night, risking the discomfort of icy streams. His origins trace back to eleventh-century England. Expect light grooming and shedding.

coat: Short, thick, close. *Colors:* black with tan markings above eyes or along sides of muzzle, and on legs and chest.

height/weight: Dog 25"–27", bitch 23"–25"/approx. 65 lbs.

behavior: A somewhat slow learner, gentle, strong-willed, wonderful with everyone, including lively children. Requires patient, firm, consistent hand in training, and must watch his diet—he loves to eat. Needs lots of outdoor exercise.

winning traits: Overall an animal that is powerful, capable, intelligent, and agile; *head* is medium long with a muzzle that is as long as the skull and the skull being almost oval; *ears* are very long, set back and low, velvet to touch; *legs*, front are straight, hind are somewhat heavily boned and well muscled, with good easy movement; *body* is strong with a straight topline and a deep chest; *tail* is natural and carried curved moderately high.

disqualify/penalize: White markings that exceed 1½" diameter, flat feet, chest that is too shallow, elbows that protrude.

considerations: Normally healthy but may develop hip dysplasia, eye and blood problems.

price range: $250–$400.

BLOODHOUND (Hound)

Writings from the third century B.C. refer to the ancestors of the Bloodhound. This outstanding tracking dog has been used also for tracking criminals; in fact, he is the only dog whose evidence is accepted in a court of law. Despite his massiveness and intimidating voice, he is very gentle. Expect moderate grooming.

coat: Short, smooth, thick. *Colors:* black and tan, red and tan, and tawny, sometimes flecked with white.

height/weight: Dog 25"–27"/90 lbs., bitch 23"–25"/80 lbs.

behavior: A slow learner, loves everyone, including active children. Strong-willed, gentle, may tend to roam and bay more than other dogs. Though an outstanding tracker, he cannot be made to attack. Needs lots of outdoor exercise.

winning traits: Overall a very strong animal that has an air of composed self-confidence; *head* is narrow and long with wrinkled, loose skin and hanging flews; *ears* are very long, velvet to touch, and low-set; *legs,* front are straight, heavy-boned and very strong, hindquarters have very muscular hips and the legs are well bent for free, easy movement; *body* is strong and solid; *tail* is thick, round and tapering.

disqualify/penalize: None.

considerations: Normally healthy but may develop digestive problems, hip dysplasia, and turned-in eyelids.

price range: $325–$450.

BORDER TERRIER (Terrier)

Used for hunting in England and Scotland, this small dog must be fast enough to keep up with a horse but small enough to follow a fox. He is very wiry and strong—a big dog in a small package. Though rare in the United States, he makes a wonderful pet. Expect little necessary grooming, with light stripping and shedding.

coat: Short, thick, and wiry. *Colors:* red, grizzle, tan, blue and tan, or wheaten, a little white on chest permissible.

height/weight: Approx. 12″/dog 13–15½ lbs., bitch 11½–14 lbs.

behavior: A quick learner, loves everyone, including children and other dogs. Gentle, obedient, wonderful all-around companion. Needs daily outdoor exercise.

winning traits: Overall a small animal with a brave, determined appearance and an "otter" head; *head* broad with a flat skull, short, full muzzle and otterlike appearance; *ears* V-shaped, set just below the top of the skull and to the side of the head; *legs*, front are somewhat widely set, straight and well boned, hind are muscular; *body* is deep-chested and has a strong back without a dip behind the shoulders; *tail* is natural but short and is carried high when animated.

disqualify/penalize: Dip behind shoulders, curly or wavy hair, white marks on feet.

considerations: Normally healthy, but may have skin prob-

lems during flea season, and some animals are prone to heart condition.
price range: $175–$250.

BORZOI (Hound)

Previously called the Russian Wolfhound, this breed is aristocratic, elegant, strong, and fast, and able to withstand the rigors of severe winters. Fluid, free, and graceful animals, they have been used as hunters of wild game. Expect moderate grooming. Shedding in dogs is normally moderate, heavy in bitches.

coat: Silky and long on the body, short on the head, ears and front of legs. *Colors:* all white or white with fawn, tan, gray, or brindle, but any color is acceptable.

height/weight: Dog 28″–31″/75–105 lbs., bitch 26″–29″/60–85 lbs.

behavior: A quick learner, gentle and likable with adults and considerate children. Somewhat aloof, can be strong-minded. Normally inactive indoors, needs lots of outdoor exercise.

winning traits: Overall it looks like an animal with tremendous speed, strength, and endurance even when it's standing still; *head* is long and very narrow with a skull that is somewhat domed and Roman-nosed; *ears* are small and set far back on head, even lying along neck when animal is relaxed; *legs*, front are straight and somewhat light, hind are long, strong, and free-moving; *body* has a deep narrow chest and a long back that rises slightly toward the loin; *tail* is natural, low, and graceful.

disqualify/penalize: Round, full, or staring eyes, light-colored eyes, elbows turned in or out.

considerations: Prone to digestive and eye problems, can be very sensitive to drugs such as those used to fight fleas.

price range: $450 and up.

BOSTON TERRIER
(Nonsporting)

This breed is truly American, developed in the United States from the English Bulldog and the English Terrier. Though originally bred to fight, they have evolved into wonderful companions. Even the most fastidious homes will welcome these animals; they shed very little and need very little grooming.

coat: Short, smooth, fine. *Colors:* brindle or black with white markings.

height/weight: Three classes (none to exceed 25 lbs.)—lightweight, under 15 lbs.; middleweight, 15–20 lbs.; heavyweight, 20–25 lbs.

behavior: A very quick learner, intelligent and alert to everything, gentle, likes everyone including children. May snore and wheeze. Good in apartment settings or in country, needs a moderate amount of exercise.

winning traits: Overall a compact dog with an alert and very intelligent presentation; *head* is flat and square without wrinkles, eyes are set wide apart, with muzzle that is broad and deep, and shorter than it is wide; *ears* are set on corners and are cropped or naturally bat-shaped; *legs*, front are short, strong, and wide-set, hind are straight when seen from behind and have muscular thighs; *body* has a deep, wide brisket and short, strong loins; *tail* is short, low-set, and carried no higher than back.

disqualify/penalize: Light-colored or walleyes, protruding teeth or jaw, long tail or one that is curled against body, solid colors, docked tail, coat that is too long or too silky, skull that is domed.

considerations: Prone to breathing problems and eye lacerations.

price range: $200–$300.

BOUVIER DES FLANDRES
(Herding)

The word *bouvier* means cow herder or ox herder in France. Bouviers are not used solely for herding, however; they are good guard dogs and general-purpose animals. Compact and powerful, they were used as messengers during World War I. Expect moderate grooming and a lot of trimming requiring a professional hand.

coat: Outercoat shaggy, wiry, rough, with a thick beard and moustache, undercoat soft and thick. *Colors:* black, salt and pepper, gray, brindle, fawn, white spot on chest permissible.

height/weight: Dog 23½"–27½", bitch at least 22¾"/approx. 70 lbs.

behavior: A very quick learner, obedient, may be aloof with strangers, but with his family he is wonderful with both adults and children. Needs lots of outdoor exercise but can adjust well to city living if exercised enough.

winning traits: Overall a short-coupled dog that is very strong, agile, and intelligent; *head* is somewhat long, flat, bearded, and has a strong wide muzzle and jaws; *ears* are high-set and erect, can be cropped or natural, if cropped should be triangular and left to make a balanced line with the head; *legs* are straight, muscular, parallel, and have very well developed thighs; *body* is short, with great power, and has a deep, wide chest and short, strong loin; *tail* is docked, short, and high-set

disqualify/penalize: Light-colored or staring eyes, nose that is brown, pink, or spotted, narrow or pointed muzzle, soft or woolly coat, chocolate brown, white or parti-colored animals, viciousness or shyness.

considerations: Normally healthy but may develop hip dysplasia and digestive problems.

price range: $200–$300.

BOXER (Working)

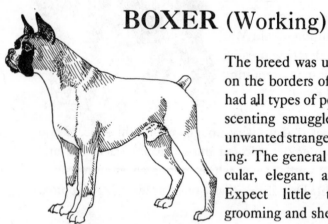

The breed was used originally on the borders of Germany. It had all types of police duties—scenting smugglers, attacking unwanted strangers, and guarding. The general build is muscular, elegant, and beautiful. Expect little to moderate grooming and shedding.

coat: Short, smooth, lying tight to body. *Colors:* fawn or brindle with small amounts of white.

height/weight: Dog 22½"–25"/66 lbs., bitch 21"–23½"/62 lbs.

behavior: A very quick learner, an outstanding guard dog but likes everyone, exceptionally good with children. Can be stubborn, outgoing, some are timid. May be sensitive to cold.

winning traits: Overall should be an alert, intelligent animal with hard muscles that are very well defined; *head* has a short nose, undershot jaw, broad, powerfully muscled muzzle, and a somewhat rounded skull; *ears* are cropped somewhat long and are erect; *legs*, front are straight and strong, hindquarters have broad hips and very powerful thighs; *body* has a deep brisket and a slightly sloping back and strong loin; *tail* is docked and carried high.

disqualify/penalize: Plump, bulldog appearance, light bone, lacking an air of nobility, uneven bite, excess skin around throat (dewlap), roach back or a back that is too lean, chest that is too wide, shallow, or deep, elbows that turn out, tail that is too low-set, any color but fawn or brindle or white (white exceeding one third of ground color).

considerations: Prone to digestive problems, may develop tumors.

price range: $250–$400.

BRIARD (Herding)

Developed in France as sheepdogs, these energetic, cheerful animals have been used also to herd cattle and as pack animals for munitions in wartime. Their hearing is very acute, and they do not bark often. Expect moderate grooming (may tend to mat) and light shedding.

coat: Long, shaggy, coarse with a fine undercoat. *Colors:* any except white, darker colors preferred.

height/weight: Dog 23"–27", bitch 22"–25½"/approx. 70 lbs.

behavior: May be a slow learner, aloof with strangers but devoted to family and children. May be single-minded and headstrong, but normally easygoing. Needs lots of outdoor exercise.

winning traits: Overall a large, powerful animal that has strength and stamina to work hard; *head* is somewhat long with a wide square muzzle; *ears*, high-set, cropped or natural, giving a square look to the head; *legs* very strongly muscled and boned, parallel, with lithe, powerful movement; *body* is wide with a deep chest and a straight back sloping up to withers from tail; *tail* is natural, long, and curved with a crook at the end.

disqualify/penalize: White or spotted coat, rump too sloping or straight, white spot on chest or feet, tail that is cut or nonexistent or carried over back, spotted or yellow eyes, short hair on head or face, spots in coat.

considerations: Prone to digestive problems, heart disorders, tumors, eye problems, and hip dysplasia.

price range: $450–$600.

BRITTANY SPANIEL
(Sporting)

The breed is characterized by ruggedness, perseverance, and agility. Generally very strong and energetic, it is a favorite gundog in Belgium, France, and Germany. In hunting, it will point a bird and endeavor to keep it from escaping until the hunter nears. Needs moderate grooming and trimming, may require a professional hand.

coat: Thick, wavy, flat. *Colors:* dark orange and white, or liver and white.

height/weight: 17½"–20½"/30–40 lbs.

behavior: A quick learner, likes everyone including children. Mild-mannered, obeys readily, very intelligent, easily trained. Has a desire to roam, needs lots of outdoor exercise.

winning traits: Overall a long-legged, strong animal that is very fast and alert; *head* has medium width and length and a straight, tapered muzzle, and eyes inset into skull to protect from briars and dirt; *ears* are covered with thick hair, hang but are set high (above eye level); *legs*, front are long, straight, and supple, hind have bent stifles for speed; *body* has a short, straight back tapering slightly down to the rump, deep chest, full flanks, and muscular thighs; *tail* is natural or docked but no more than 4" long.

disqualify/penalize: Black or colors that are too pale, too much feathering, nose that is too heavy, snipy, or Roman, black nose, two-colored nose, light-colored eyes, flappy or pendulous lips, tendency to drool, narrow chest, crooked elbows or legs, over/undersized animals, tail longer than four inches, back that is too long.

considerations: Normally healthy but may develop hip dysplasia and can have eye problems.

price range: $200–$300.

BRUSSELS GRIFFON (Toy)

This breed originated in Belgium, where the word *griffon* means thick-haired. Originally they were ratters but later were developed into companions for the wealthy. Their expression is quite bright and humanlike. The smooth variety requires little grooming; the rough coated needs moderate grooming and professional trimming.

coat: Either rough or smooth. *Colors:* red-brown, if rough coated some black or solid black is allowed; if coat is smooth, solid black is not allowed.

height/weight: Approx 8"/8–12 lbs.

behavior: A very quick learner, alert, can be very strong-willed and nervous, is intelligent enough to manipulate owner. May bark a lot Very active in and out of doors.

winning traits: Overall a sturdy, thick-set animal with a smart athletic look; *head* is large and rounded with a very short, black nose; *ears* are high-set and can be cropped or natural, if cropped will be almost erect; *legs* are medium-long, strong, well-muscled, parallel; *body* has a deep, wide brisket and a short back; *tail* is docked.

disqualify/penalize: Pink or spotted nose, any white spot in coat, tongue that hangs, overshot jaw, black color in the smooth variety.

considerations: Bitches may be difficult to breed and litters may be small, prone to eye and breathing problems and slipped stifle.

price range: $400–$500.

BULLDOG (Nonsporting)

Originally used to fight bulls, these dogs were bred for extraordinary strength and courage. These contests were eventually outlawed, and in a few generations the breed's original viciousness was bred out, leaving us with one of the finest of family dogs. Needs only moderate grooming, little shedding.

coat: Straight, flat, close, fine, shiny, smooth. *Colors:* bright brindle of any color, white, solid red or fawn or creamy yellow, piebald.

height/weight: 15″/dog 50 lbs., bitch 40 lbs.

behavior: A somewhat slow learner, loves everyone and is very good with children. Outgoing, can be stubborn and bold. Needs a fair amount of outdoor exercise.

winning traits: Overall a heavy dog with a huge head and a wide, low-set body; *head* is wrinkled and massive, from the front view is high, broad, and square, in profile is high and short with a flat forehead, muzzle has hanging flews and huge undershot jaws; *ears* are small, wide-set, and high, with rose ear the most desirable shape; *legs*, front are wide-set, very muscular, and straight, looking bowed because of muscles (not because of bone), hind are longer than front and are straight when seen from behind; *body* is very wide, deep-chested, and has a short back that is lower behind the shoulders than it is over the withers but curving up again at the tail (a roach back); *tail* is low-set and can be straight, bent, or kinked.

disqualify/penalize: Flesh-colored or brown nose, legginess.
considerations: Normally healthy, may be short-lived, bothered by hot weather, may have allergies and be prone to eye disorders and hip dysplasia.
price range: $400–$500.

BULLMASTIFF (Working)

These fearless animals are extremely strong, agile, fast, and quiet. A cross between the Mastiff and the Bulldog, they were bred in England as "gamekeepers' night dogs" to guard deer and game from poachers. Needs moderate grooming, also expect moderate shedding.

coat: Short, flat, dense. *Colors:* brindle, fawn or red, small white spot on chest acceptable.
height/weight: Dog 25"–27"/110–130 lbs., bitch 24"–26"/100–120 lbs.
behavior: A very quick learner, may be aloof with strangers. Devoted to his family, but should be introduced to children as a puppy. Can be aggressive (if an animal is aggressive, its strength may make it dangerous to walk and control). May be inactive indoors but needs lots of outdoor exercise.
winning traits: Overall a giant that gives the impression of great but gentle power; *head* is very large and wide with wrinkles and a flat forehead; *ears* are set back on head and wide so they give a square look to the head; *legs* are wide-set, muscular,

and straight when seen from behind or head-on; *body* has a brisket that is deep and wide with broad hips that are powerfully muscled; *tail* is natural, either curved or straight and not carried too high.

disqualify/penalize: White anywhere other than chest, cowhocks, or splayed feet.

considerations: May be short-lived, prone to hip dysplasia, eyelids that turn in, digestive problems, boils, tends to snore and drool.

price range: $400–$500.

BULL TERRIER (Terrier)

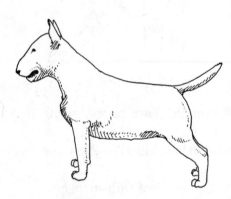

The breed was developed in England to excel as a fearless fighting dog; for his size he is the strongest of all Terriers. Since the sport became illegal, he has been bred to be a good companion, and with training he can be shown competitively and peacefully. Expect moderate grooming and shedding.

coat: Short, harsh, lying flat to body. *Colors:* two varieties, the all white, or the colored, which can be any other color (brindle is preferred) with white chest, feet, and blaze.

height/weight: 12″–18″/39½–48½ lbs.

behavior: A slow learner, aloof with strangers, good companion for adults. Because of background as a fighting dog, may be quarrelsome with strange dogs unless well trained and socialized at an early age. Needs constant, patient training to overcome stubbornness and short concentration. Needs lots of outdoor exercise.

winning traits: Overall is powerfully built and big-boned with an intense but sweet demeanor; *head* from front view is oval, in profile it is long and has flat forehead, long muzzle and shorter skull; *ears* are small, placed toward back of skull, erect and held close together; *legs* large-boned, moderately long, and parallel from front or back view, with powerfully muscled thighs; *body* is rounded with short, strong back and a slight rise from chest to belly; *tail* natural, short and low-set (almost horizontal).

disqualify/penalize: Blue or pink eyes, in the colored variety a predominantly white color.

considerations: Normally healthy but is prone to deafness, tends to snore.

price range: $250 and up.

CAIRN TERRIER (Terrier)

This breed, with its naturally bright and foxy appearance, was developed in Scotland and brought to the United States in 1913. They are frisky, hardy, active hunters, and their double coat makes them suited to all types of weather. The coat, however, demands very little effort; it needs little grooming, and shedding is limited.

coat: Outercoat is coarse and thick, undercoat short and soft. *Colors:* any except white; ears, muzzle, and tip of tail are preferred in dark colors.

height/weight: Dog 10″/14 lbs., bitch 9½″/13 lbs.

behavior: A very quick learner, devoted to his family, may be aloof with strangers. Tends to be strong-willed and outgoing, energetic, active, loyal, and good with adults. An excellent choice for apartment dwelling but will require some outdoor exercise.

winning traits: Overall a short-legged animal that is somewhat long in the body and has an alert, eager expression; *head* is wide with strong muzzle that tends to shortness; *ears* are erect, small, and wide-set on head; *legs* are moderately boned and straight, front feet may turn out slightly; *body* is strong, with a straight medium-long back; *tail* is natural, set level with back and is gay (but not over back), giving balance in relationship to head.

disqualify/penalize: Over/undershot jaw, eyes that are ringed, yellow, or too large, white on body, flesh-colored nose, back too short or compact, low-set tail, thin feet, crooked legs, ears that are too closely set, too large, carried too high, or too furry, head that is too narrow.

considerations: None.

price range: $300–$400.

CHESAPEAKE BAY RETRIEVER (Sporting)

This fellow is the quintessential breed for hunting in all weather. His coat is well oiled and sheds water quickly while retaining body heat. He loves water, is intelligent and alert, strong and eager, and loves to work. Expect moderate grooming and shedding.

coat: Thick and short (not more than 1½″ long), straight with a little wave over shoulders. *Colors:* any shade of brown to faded tan (colors that blend with the outdoors), white on chest and toes permissible.

height/weight: Dog 23″–26″/65–75 lbs., bitch 21″–24″/55–65 lbs.

behavior: A somewhat slow learner, is an excellent one-family guard dog, very good with children. Normally mild-mannered, but can be strong-willed, needs firm training at an early age; if trained properly is a loyal, sweet companion. Needs quite a lot of outdoor exercise.

winning traits: Overall is bright, strong, and energetic; *head* is broad with a round skull and a medium-length muzzle that is somewhat pointed, with clean lips (not hanging loose); *ears* are small, hanging, and set high on head; *legs* are well muscled, parallel, and hindquarters are powerful; *body* is medium-long, muscular, and powerful and has a broad, deep chest and moderately high flanks; *tail* is as long as hocks, straight and feathered.

disqualify/penalize: Black color, white anywhere but on breast, stomach, or toes, dewclaws on hind legs, over/undershot jaw, curly coat, tail with feathers more than 1¾″ long.

considerations: May be prone to skin problems (eczema) and hip dysplasia.

price range: $250–$400.

CHIHUAHUA (Toy)

CHIHUAHUA: SMOOTH COAT

Worshipped in ancient times, this line dates back to ninth-century Mexico. Long-lived, it is now not only the smallest but also one of the top-ranked breeds in the United States. They like their own kind but rarely get along with other breeds. Expect light shedding and little grooming.

coat: Two types—smooth, soft, close, and shiny, or longer with a soft undercoat. *Colors*. any color is permissible.

height/weight: Approx. 5″/1–6 lbs.

behavior: A very quick learner, is normally aloof with strangers, and is a one-man dog. Can be timid, high-strung but gentle. May bark more than most breeds. Does not need a lot of outdoor exercise but is very active even indoors.

winning traits: Overall is a tiny, compact animal with a delicate intelligent look; *head* is round with an apple dome and a short nose that comes to a point; *ears* are large in proportion to head, erect when animal is alert, and on long-coated variety will have a light fringe; *legs*, front are straight and fine, hindquarters have well-muscled thighs with legs that are straight when seen from behind; *body* has a straight back that is somewhat long; *tail* is natural and carried high with a gentle curve over the back (a sickle tail).

disqualify/penalize: Droopy or broken-down ears, cropped tail or a tail that is low or tucked under, thin coat in the long-haired variety.

considerations: May be sensitive to the cold, prone to rheumatism, nervousness, colds, gum diseases, epilepsy.

price range: $250–$400.

CHIHUAHUA: ROUGH COAT

CHOW CHOW (Nonsporting)

One of the best guard dogs, its ancestry traces back to the China of two thousand years ago. Only they and the Sharpeis are known to have a blue-black tongue. One of the most fastidious breeds, it may be the easiest to housebreak. Requires considerable grooming, some upkeep with shedding.

coat: Outercoat straight, profuse, thick, protruding; undercoat soft and woolly. *Colors:* any solid color with lighter shading on the ruff, hind, and tail.

height/weight: Minimum 18"/approx. 60 lbs.

behavior: A very quick, alert learner, somewhat aloof, even with owner, and should be introduced to family when quite young. Can be strong-willed and cantankerous at times, must be trained with a firm, controlled hand. Calm and inactive indoors, but needs daily outdoor exercise.

winning traits: Overall a short-coupled, proud animal with an enormous head showing great power and natural beauty; *head* is huge, wide, and flat with a short muzzle and full lips; *ears* are wide-set and high, small, and tipped forward slightly; *legs* are heavy-boned and straight when seen from front or back; *body* is compact and short; *tail* is carried high and over back.

disqualify/penalize: Nose any color but black (except in the blue Chow, whose nose can be solid blue or slate), red, pink, or spotted tongue, drop ear or ears.

considerations: Normally healthy but may be prone to turned-in eyelids, ear infections, and can be bothered by hot weather.

price range: $400–$500.

CLUMBER SPANIEL
(Sporting)

This dog comes from England, where weight standards for the breed are heavier than in the United States. The breed is very dignified and may work slowly but is probably the most easily trained of the Spaniels. When given a hunting pace that is not hurried, he makes an excellent shooting dog. Expect moderate grooming and trimming that may require professional skill. Sheds moderately.

coat: Straight, silky, thick, soft, long, with feathers. *Colors:* beautiful lemon yellow and white, or orange and white.

height/weight: 17″–18″/dog 55–65 lbs., bitch 35–50 lbs.

behavior: A somewhat slow learner, loves everyone and is especially tolerant with children. Gentle, loving, may be somewhat strong-willed. Needs outdoor exercise but is not too active indoors.

winning traits: Appears heavy with very strong, methodical movement; *head* is very heavy and flat with a strong brow and square muzzle; *ears* hang and are wide-set at about eye level; *legs*, front are short, heavy, and straight, back are very well muscled and on broad hips; *body* is very strong and deep with a wide chest, straight back and loins, and a long neck with some looseness of skin; *tail* is docked and carried merrily.

disqualify/penalize: None.

considerations: Normally healthy but may develop hip dysplasia, easily becomes fat, may drool and snore.
price range: $300–$400.

COCKER SPANIEL (Sporting)

Probably the most popular breed in the world, the Cocker is enthusiastic and eager to please. Originally used in hunting woodcock in England (from which the name derives), it is still used for flushing and retrieving. Grooming and trimming are essential and require a professional hand. Expect moderate shedding.

coat: Wavy and thick (never curly) on body, short and fine on the head. *Colors:* black, red-cream, buff, liver, as well as mixtures of black and white, and black and tan.
height/weight: Dog 15½", bitch under 14½"/22–28 lbs.
behavior: A very quick learner, normally sweet and gentle, loving everyone including children. (Puppy mills, however, have bred animals that are excitable, nervous, and sickly—best to know your breeder well before commitment to any animal.)
winning traits: Overall a fairly small animal that is fast and has a beautifully balanced silhouette; *head* has a skull that is round with full, square lips and a definite stop, length of muzzle is the same as the length of the skull bone, head is set on a long, muscular neck and carried proudly; *ears* are long, silky, and

hang from a point that begins about eye level; *legs*, front are straight and strong, hind have muscular thighs and a good angulation in the stifle; *body* is compact and strong with a back that slopes down slightly from the withers and has a deep chest; *tail* is docked and carried merrily.

disqualify/penalize: White markings anywhere but on chest and throat on the solid-colored varieties; on the parti-colored variety any color dominating more than 90 percent of body, tan markings covering more than 10 percent of body, heights in excess of standards.

considerations: May develop cataracts, hemophilia, slipped stifle (knee), or be prone to indigestion and trouble with ears.

price range: $250–$400.

COLLIE (Herding)

COLLIE: ROUGH COAT

The collie was little known until a century ago, when Queen Victoria became enamored of him. Originally bred to herd sheep in Scotland, he is now used mostly as a wonderful and elegant companion. Grooming varies with the long- and short-coated varieties. With the longer-coated Rough Collie, expect to spend several hours per week, with heavy shedding. In the short-coated Smooth Collie, grooming and shedding are moderate.

coat: Two types—smooth variety is hard, thick, and smooth; rough-coated has a long, thick outercoat and undercoat on the body but not on the head and legs. *Colors:* sable and white, tricolor, mostly black, white, blue merle (mottled blue, grey, and black).

height/weight: Dog 24"–26"/60–75 lbs., bitch 22"–24"/50–65 lbs.

behavior: A very quick learner, most lines are gentle with everyone, adults as well as children. Normally obedient and easily trained, some lines can tend to be nippy and aloof and may be impatient with children. Needs a lot of outdoor exercise.

winning traits: Overall a slender, active animal with a lively animated personality; *head* is long, slim, wedge-shaped, and flat; *ears* must be in proportion to the head, with a characteristic fold toward the tip when held erect, folded back onto the ruff when relaxed; *legs* are parallel with strong muscle and bone and small feet, movement is graceful and reaching; *body* is somewhat long and muscular with a deep brisket and strong, straight back; *tail* is long and low-set when relaxed, curved and alert when dog is animated.

disqualify/penalize: Over/undershot jaw, low or prick ears, large, round, or full eyes, rough dogs without undercoat, dogs with cowhocks or straight stifles, curly outer coat, over/undersized animal.

considerations: May be prone to detached retina, tip of nose may be sensitive to sun or easily bruised, can have a sickness called Gray Collie syndrome as a puppy.

price range: $350 and up.

COLLIE: SMOOTH COAT

CURLY-COATED RETRIEVER (Sporting)

Although one of the best hunting dogs in the world, this breed is extremely rare in the United States. They love the water, are tireless in it, and are especially adept at retrieving downed waterfowl. The origins of the curly coat remain a mystery. Expect light grooming and moderate shedding.

coat: Massed curls all over. *Color:* black or liver
height/weight: Approx. 24"/70–80 lbs.
behavior: A quick learner, loves everyone including children. Easygoing, may be shy, so early training with family is important. Needs lots of outdoor activity.
winning traits: Overall is a strong, intelligent animal covered with tight curls; *head* is somewhat long with clean lips; *ears* are small and hanging; *legs* are moderately long, front are straight and hindquarters are muscular; *body* is somewhat short and well muscled with a deep chest; *tail* is natural with curls
disqualify/penalize: Saddleback, uncurled hair over shoulders, white patch on chest.
considerations: May be prone to hip dysplasia.
price range: $200–$300

DACHSHUND (Hound)

The breed was used originally to hunt badgers in Germany because they dig so well. Their popularity now is due to their desirability as clean, bright, and alert companions. Grooming ranges from light with the shorthaired, moderate with the long-haired, to almost daily for the wirehaired (which also needs stripping).

DACHSHUND: SMOOTH

coat: Three types—smooth, wirehaired, or long-haired. *Colors:* smooth (or shorthaired) are solid red, yellow, brindle, or black, chocolate, gray with tan markings; long- and wirehairs permit all colors, white spot on chest permissible.

height/weight: 9″–10″/dog, up to 25 lbs.; bitch, up to 23 lbs.; miniature, less than 10 lbs.

behavior: A very quick learner, devoted to family, may be aloof with strangers. Alert, can be strong-willed and assertive, may be impatient with children. May bark a lot, very active.

winning traits: Overall a very long, low animal with strength and intelligence; *head* is clean with a tapered muzzle and a slightly domed skull; *ears* are high-set, rounded, and hang so that front edge touches cheek; *legs* are very short, muscular, and somewhat turned inward, hindquarters are well muscled; *body* has a straight back and deep chest, with a strong breastbone and slightly tucked-up abdomen; *tail* is natural with a gentle curve and is carried as an extension of the back.

disqualify/penalize: Over/undershot jaw, loose shoulders, legs too long, body hanging between the shoulders, waddle, turned in/out toes, sunken back, short-ribbed or weak chest, flanks too high, narrow weak hindquarters, bowed legs, wall eyes (except in dapple dogs).

considerations: May be prone to spinal problems.

price range: $300 and up.

DACHSHUND: WIREHAIRED

DACHSHUND: LONG-HAIRED

DALMATIAN (Nonsporting)

At one time the Dalmatian was used as a follower and guardian of horse-drawn coaches; to this day he has an unusual affinity for horses. He has an incredible memory and is truly a multi-use animal: hunter, companion, and shepherd, and at one time a war dog and a guard dog. Expect moderate grooming and shedding.

coat: Short, shiny, fine, thick, sleek. *Colors:* ground color of white with spots of black or liver.

height/weight: 19″–23″/dog approx. 55 lbs., bitch 50 lbs.

behavior: A quick learner, very active, a one-family dog, best as the companion of adults. Easily trained, may be timid, so early introduction to family is best.

winning traits: Overall a medium-sized, muscular animal that has strength and stamina and an outgoing way; *head* is moderately long, flat, and wide between the ears, the muzzle is long, clean, and strong; *ears* are high-set on head, broad at the root, and taper to round at the end; *legs* are straight when seen from front or back, heavy-boned, and give a straight, reaching gait; *tail* is moderately long (about to hocks) and slightly curved.

disqualify/penalize: Specked or flesh-colored nose, cow hocks, flat feet, shyness, absence of pigment in rims of eyes, unnatural position of eyelashes, tail that is carried up over back or is too low-set, under/overshot jaw, colors or sizes not mentioned above.

considerations: May become deaf or blind, prone to skin and kidney problems.

price range: $300–$400

DANDIE DINMONT TERRIER (Terrier)

These Terriers took their name from a character in a novel by Sir Walter Scott They were first recognized around 1700 between England and Scot land, where they hunted otters and badgers Their soft-eyed look may be a fooler; they are strong-willed and seem to have an opinion about everything. Expect several hours a month of grooming and stripping with a professional hand. Tends to shed moderately

coat: Mixture of hard and soft, about 2″ long almost every-where. *Colors.* mustard, bluish black or gray, normally with some white on chest, white claws acceptable.

height/weight: 8″–11″/18–24 lbs.

behavior: A very quick learner, can be stubborn, may be impatient with children. A one-family dog with a strong per-sonality. Fairly active both in and outdoors, needs some out-door exercise.

winning traits: Overall a small animal with a long body and very large head; *head* is large and broad with a domed skull; *ears* hang, are set low and back on head, and have a small fringe of hair at the tips; *legs*, front are heavy-boned, short, very muscular and wide-set, hind are somewhat longer than front and have very muscular thighs; *body* is limber, long, muscular with a deep chest; *tail* is natural, curved and somewhat short.

disqualify/penalize: Twisted or curled tail, flat feet, wiry hair.

considerations: May be prone to back and kidney problems, can snore more than other breeds.

price range: $400 and up.

DOBERMAN PINSCHER
(Working)

This one gives the impression of being a blue-blooded aristocrat. He is very adaptable and has been used in many different ways: as a guard dog, a criminal tracker, a shepherd, and a guide dog for the blind. He is a devoted family member. His musculature is so dense that he can be mistaken for a dog fifteen to twenty pounds lighter. Expect moderate grooming and shedding.

coat: Close-lying, hard, thick, smooth. *Colors:* black, red, blue, fawn, with rust markings above eyes, on muzzle, throat, feet, legs, chest, and below tail.

height/weight: Dog 26″–28″/67–75 lbs., bitch 24″–26″/57–65 lbs.

behavior: Breed seems prone to two extremes—one is a very quick learner, active, good with adults and children if introduced to family when very young; the other can be vicious, timid, fearful, difficult to train. Know your breeder well. Active in/outdoors, needs lots of outdoor exercise.

winning traits: Overall a medium-sized animal with an alert, intelligent demeanor; *head* is long, wedge-shaped, and flat with a long, clean, muscled muzzle; *ears* are normally cropped but can be left natural, root of ear is about level with highest part of skull; *legs*, front are straight and heavy-boned, hind are on fairly broad hips and are somewhat straight, giving free movement; *body* has a short, straight back with wide, deep chest and muscled loins; *tail* is docked and held erect when animal is alert.

disqualify/penalize: Shyness, viciousness, over/undershot jaw, four or more missing teeth, glassy or slit eyes, coarse or fine (greyhound) build, over/undersized, head out of balance with body.

considerations: Normally healthy but may be sensitive to cold, prone to bloat, hip dysplasia, eye problems, and hypothyroidism.

price range: $300 and up.

ENGLISH COCKER SPANIEL (Sporting)

If any breed can be said to have a sense of humor, it is this one. In spite of his name, his origins are in Spain, where he was developed into a superior flushing and retrieving dog. He is a "people" dog and is truly happy with companionship anywhere. Expect moderate to heavy grooming and trimming. Sheds moderately.

coat: Medium length, wavy and silky on body, short and fine on head. *Colors:* vary from solid black to solid white, and include parti-color.

height/weight: Dog 16"–17"/28–34 lbs., bitch 15"–16"/26–32 lbs.

behavior: A very quick learner, loves everyone, including children, devoted to his family. Fun-loving, lively, easygoing. Is somewhat active even indoors, needs a lot of outdoor exercise.

winning traits: Overall appears alert, lively, and happy, with strong, free movement and an unmistakably intelligent look; *head* has a high, arched forehead and a strong square muzzle about the same length as the skull; *ears* are long, low-set, and silky; *legs*, front are straight and strong, hind have thighs that are round, broad, strong, and well-bent in the stifles; *body* is strong and compact, with a short back that slopes downward to the tail, and a strong loin and deep chest; *tail* is gay and carried as an extension of the back.

disqualify/penalize: Light-colored, round, or protruding eyes, muzzle that is too short or snipy, dewlap, short or thick neck, feet that are too small or too large or toes that are too spreading, under or over size, long or sway back or roach back, tail that is too low/high or that is too short/long.

considerations: May develop hip dysplasia and have eye or ear problems.

price range: $150–$300.

ENGLISH FOXHOUND
(Hound)

These animals are very graceful and strong. As the name suggests, they excel in fox hunting because of their superior nose and endurance. They are so rare as pets that they almost appear to be resisting domestication. They need little to moderate grooming and will shed lightly.

coat: Short, glossy, thick. *Colors:* black, tan, white, or any combination of these colors.

height/weight: Approx. 23"/70–75 lbs.

behavior: Breed is so rare in the United States that there is little known about it. Likely, however, to be too independent to be a companion pet. Needs lots of outdoor exercise.

winning traits: Overall a well-balanced animal that is somewhat heavier boned than the American Foxhound; *head* is ample but not heavy and has a long nose; *ears* are low-set, typical hanging hound's ears; *legs* are very straight and heavy boned with catlike feet; *body* is strong with a very straight back; *tail* is natural and carried high (not over back) with a slight curve.

disqualify/penalize: Over/undershot jaw.
considerations: None
price range: The breed is so rare in the United States there are no price guidelines.

ENGLISH SETTER (Sporting)

As hunters they excel at finding birds, pointing them, and then "setting" until the hunter ap proaches to catch them. Their appearance is beautiful and aristocratic, with a smooth, graceful carriage and move ment. Expect somewhat heavy grooming and trimming that re quires a skillful hand. Sheds moderately

coat: Fairly long and flat without curl. *Colors:* black, white, and tan, lemon or orange or liver and white, liver or lemon or orange belton (two colors on one hair), all white, with preference given to dogs with flecked colors rather than heavy patches of color.
height/weight: Dog 25″, bitch 24″/50–70 lbs.
behavior: May be a slow learner, loves everyone, including children. Easygoing, placid, gentle, strong-willed, early train

ing is best. Quite inactive indoors, but needs a lot of outdoor exercise, city living acceptable if exercised enough.

winning traits: Overall graceful and agile, with refined carriage and flowing lines; *head* is moderately wide with a long and lean profile, muzzle also long and square, with flews that hang somewhat; *ears* are low, set back on head, and silky; *legs*, front are straight and strong, hind are strong with good, straight movement; *body* has a straight back or one with little downward slope from the withers, hips are wide and loin is strong, chest is deep and somewhat narrow; *tail* is about as long as the hocks, is feathered, and tapers to a point.

disqualify/penalize: Stilted or lumbering gait, bushy tail, soft or woolly coat.

considerations: May roam, prone to hip dysplasia.

price range: $250–$300.

ENGLISH SPRINGER SPANIEL (Sporting)

These are the oldest of the Spaniels and are as popular today as they were four hundred years ago. As hunters they are fast, and because they flush game well they are considered superior pheasant dogs. Expect a fair amount of grooming and experienced trimming. Sheds moderately.

coat: Medium length on body, flat or wavy, dense enough to be weatherproof and thornproof, short on head and front of forelegs. *Colors:* liver or black with white markings, liver and white with tan or blue or liver roan or white predominating, black, liver, or tan markings.

height/weight: Dog 20″, bitch 19″/45–55 lbs.

behavior: A quick learner, gentle with everybody, loves children, very devoted to his family. Easygoing and normally obedient, fun-loving and playful. Needs lots of outdoor exercise.

winning traits: Overall a strong, gentle, compact animal with endurance; *head* is strong, broad, flat on top, and balanced with the rest of the body, muzzle is square and strong, enabling it to carry game; *ears* are long and set in a line with eyes; *legs*, front are strong and straight with shoulders, providing good movement, hind are fully developed with strong thighs and straight legs when seen from back view; *body* is compact, muscled, deep-chested, and has a straight back with a moderate rise at the loins; *tail* is docked, happy, and held almost straight out.

disqualify/penalize: Timidity or viciousness, over or under size, legginess, excessive heaviness, colors not mentioned above, rough or curly coat, head not conforming to standards, light or yellow eyes, swayback, tail too high or low, mincing or choppy movement, splayed feet, hocks turned in or out.
considerations: May be prone to hip dysplasia, allergies, eye and ear problems, may overeat.
price range: $250–$300.

ENGLISH TOY SPANIEL
(Toy)

CAVALIER KING CHARLES SPANIEL

The breed was the darling of royalty and aristocrats for many centuries. They make excellent pets and have the talent to make good hunters. Four varieties are recognized (see below). Only moderate grooming and perhaps light trimming are required. Sheds moderately.

coat: Long, silky with soft waves and a full mane. *Colors:* different on each variety—King Charles is black with tan markings, Ruby is chestnut red, Blenheim is red and white, Prince Charles is white, black, and tan.
height/weight: Approx. 10″/9–12 lbs.
behavior: A very quick learner, may be aloof with strangers but a quiet, easygoing companion for his family, best with somewhat adult children. Happy with mild exercise.
winning traits: Overall a small animal with a proportionately

large body; *head* is strongly domed with wide-set eyes, a short, turned-up nose and deep square muzzle; *ears* are very long for a small animal, are low-set and covered with thick, wavy hair; *legs* straight when seen from front and back views, medium-long and strong; *body* is short and compact with a wide chest and a short, wide back; *tail* is docked.

disqualify/penalize: White color on the King Charles or the Ruby variety.

considerations: May be prone to respiratory problems, eye lacerations, slipped stifle (knee), may wheeze or snore.

price range: $250 and up.

FIELD SPANIEL (Sporting)

This is the rarest of the Spaniel breeds. Perhaps because it was originally bred with such an unappealingly long body, heavy bones, and short legs, it never became popular. Now, however, it has been bred to beauty and balance while retaining its talent as a fine flusher and retriever. Expect moderate grooming and skilled trimming. Sheds moderately.

coat: Thick, glossy, flat, silky. *Colors:* normally black, liver, or mahogany, but colors can vary.

height/weight: Approx. 18"/35–50 lbs.

behavior: A quick learner, mild-mannered and gentle with everyone, including children. Easily trained, eager to please, may want to roam. Active both in and out of doors, needs lots of outdoor exercise.

winning traits: Overall is a strong and enduring animal that has an even-tempered outlook; *head* is long and somewhat narrow with a long muzzle; *ears* are low-set, long, and feathered; *legs*, front are somewhat long with medium bone, hind are strong with moderately bent stifles that are straight when viewed from behind; *body* is moderately long and strong, with a strong loin; *tail* is docked.

disqualify/penalize: Stifles twisted in or out, colors other than those mentioned above.

considerations: May develop hip dysplasia, can snore.

price range: $300–$500.

FINNISH SPITZ (Nonsporting)

This is the newest breed recognized by the American Kennel Club, and they can now compete for championships. They are sight, scent, and sound hunters in their native Finland, and they make wonderful all-around pointers. Expect light to moderate grooming and heavy shedding.

coat: Double, long, and straight. *Colors:* from pale honey to auburn, with a lighter undercoat, and lighter coat on the cheeks and underside, inside the legs and ears, and on the back of the tail. Pups are normally born darker and turn adult colors as they age.

height/weight: Dog 17½″–20″, bitch 15½″–18″.

behavior: A fast learner, can be overly sensitive, somewhat aloof with strangers but devoted to its family and children. Needs lots of outdoor exercise in all kinds of weather.

winning traits: Overall a bright, foxy, very well balanced animal with a glorious golden-red coat and brisk, confident movement; *head* is moderately wide with almond-shaped eyes that tilt upward toward the outer corners to give a foxlike appearance; *ears* are erect, pointed, and high-set; *legs* are strong and straight; *body* is symmetrical and square; *tail* is plumed and about to the hocks, but beginning just below the line of the back is curled and held high over the back, adding balance to the carriage of the head.

disqualify/penalize: Ears that are set too high and too close to the top of the head, or that curve downward toward eyes when held erect, tail that is too long, too short, too curled, or too heavily furnished, any feature that is exaggerated to give an unbalanced appearance.

considerations: Normally healthy but as a pup can be prone to cleft palate and throat problems.

price range: $450–$800.

FLAT-COATED RETRIEVER
(Sporting)

As one of the best swimmers, this Retriever makes a superior water dog. Although it is one of the rarest breeds, it is an excellent pheasant hunter, one with both strength and endurance. Expect moderate grooming and shedding, and light trimming.

coat: Thick, very shiny, fine and flat. *Colors:* usually black or liver, with some white permissible.

height/weight: Approx. 23"/60–70 lbs.

behavior: A quick learner, loves everyone, including children. Easily trained, obeys readily, gentle, mild-mannered, level-headed, stable. Needs lots of outdoor exercise.

winning traits: Overall these animals should appear eager and intelligent, with an elegance that is both strong and clean; *head* is somewhat large, long and strong in order to carry game, the muzzle about the same length as the skull; *ears* are somewhat small with thick hair; *legs* are moderately long and straight in front, hind have power and muscle without excessive bone; *body* has a broad, deep chest with a muscled brisket, a long loin, and a straight back; *tail* is about the length of the hocks and is carried level with the back.

disqualify/penalize: Nervousness, aggressiveness, behavior that is hyperactive, too apathetic, shy or stubborn, fluffy, curled or wavy coat, eyes that protrude or are yellow, weak muzzle or jaw, over/undershot mouth, weak back, shallow or weak chest.

considerations: Normally healthy but can have hip dysplasia and eye and ear problems.

price range: $250 and up.

FOX TERRIER (Terrier)

There are two distinct varieties of Fox Terriers recognized by the American Kennel Club: the **Smooth** and the **Wirehaired**. Watch their tails; they tell how spunky and gay this breed is! They were once used as hunting dogs because of their keen nose and eyesight. Little grooming required in the Smooth; the Wirehaired needs professional skill with stripping and trimming. Both varieties shed little.

FOX TERRIER: SMOOTH

coat: *Smooth Fox Terrier*, smooth, thick, flat, hard; *Wirehaired Fox Terrier*, very thick, stiff, ¾″–1½″ in length. *Colors:* mostly white with other colored spots and flecks.

height/weight: Dog maximum 15½″/18 lbs., bitch maximum 12″/16 lbs.

behavior: A very quick learner, likes everyone. May be strong-willed, aggessively bold, very outgoing, may bark a lot. Needs activity everywhere, whether in or out of doors.

winning traits: Overall an alert, eager animal with button ears that fold over on top of the head; *head* is flat and somewhat narrow, with strong jaws; *ears* are small, V-shaped, with a fold high above the top line of the skull; *legs*, front are straight, hind are straight when seen from behind, both front and back are carried straight forward when in motion; *body* is short and has a straight back, deep chest, and a powerful loin with a little arch; *tail* is docked and carried high and gaily.

disqualify/penalize: Nose that is white, cherry or spotted, ears that are prick or are folded to show the inside, over/undershot jaw, red, blue, or liver colors.

considerations: None.

price range: $250 and up.

FOX TERRIER: WIREHAIRED

FRENCH BULLDOG
(Nonsporting)

In spite of its name, the breed probably originated in England. It is distinguished by its bat ears and a flat forehead that extends over its eyes. At one time they were known as the Boule-Dog Français. They require little grooming and will shed only lightly.

coat: Somewhat fine, bright, smooth, and short. *Colors:* all fawn, white, or brindle.

height/weight: Approx. 12″/19–22 lbs.

behavior: A quick learner, may be aloof with strangers, good with adults. Quiet, can be strong-willed. Can be active indoors, needs some outdoor activity.

winning traits: Overall a short, muscular animal with bat ears; *head* is big, square, flat on top with a somewhat rounded forehead and a short, broad, deep muzzle with hanging flews; *ears* are wide at the root, set high on head, and long, with the opening facing front; *legs* are wide-set, short, heavy, and strong, the hind legs longer than the front; *body* is short, compact, and rounded, with a wide, deep, ample chest, the back dips behind the shoulders and rises ahead of the tail (roach back); *tail* is short and low-set, can be straight or kinked.

disqualify/penalize: Ears that are not bat-shaped, disqualifying colors of black and white, black and tan, liver, mouse, or solid black, eyes of different colors, light-colored nose in light-colored dogs, harelip, any mutilation, weight over 28 pounds.

considerations: Prone to eye lacerations, can wheeze or snore and have breathing problems, may be uncomfortable in heat or cold.
price range: $200 and up.

GERMAN SHEPHERD
(Herding)

This is truly a working dog, and one of the most popular breeds in the United States. Their history is that of herding dogs in Germany, but they are excellent police trackers, guards, and guide dogs for the blind. In Great Britain the breed is known as the Alsatian. Expect moderate daily grooming and daily shedding.

coat: Full, thick, and double. *Colors:* most colors permissible, richer colors preferred such as black to light gray, black with tan, brindle, or gray, or gray with sable markings.
height/weight: Dog 24″–26″, bitch 22″–24″/75–85 lbs.
behavior: A very quick learner, may be aloof with strangers but is devoted to his family, excellent with children. Obedient, alert, should be trained early with a kind, consistent hand. Some are nervous and shy and may be fear-biters (animals whose immediate reaction to fear is to bite). Needs a lot of exercise.
winning traits: Overall an animal that is somewhat long, very strong, with a demeanor of poised intelligence; *head* is long with

a wedge-shaped muzzle, sloping skull and strong, well developed jaw; *ears* are natural, somewhat pointed, and erect when dog is at attention; *legs* are straight when seen from front and back, strong with oval bones and muscular thighs; *body* has a straight back that slopes gracefully up from the hips, a deep chest and wide, strong loin; *tail* is long and low-set when relaxed.

disqualify/penalize: Cropped ears or ears that hang, docked tail, undershot jaw, all-white animals, nose that is not mostly black, dog that tries to bite the judge!

considerations: May be prone to digestive problems, dwarfism, and heart disease, must be watched very closely for hip dysplasia (best to make sure dam and sire have been OFA certified clear of it). Knowing your breeder is especially important with this breed to ensure you get the type of animal you want.

price range: $350–$500.

GERMAN SHORTHAIRED POINTER (Sporting)

This dog was bred to be an all-around hunting dog. He is used as a retriever from land and water, and he points as well. He has excellent endurance and is a good dog close to the gun. His short hair he requires light grooming, and he will shed moderately.

coat: Tough, hard, short, thick enough to stand rigorous weather. *Colors:* liver, liver and white spotted and/or ticked, roan.

height/weight: Dog 23"–25"/55–70 lbs., bitch 21"–23"/45–60 lbs.

behavior: A quick learner, devoted, gentle, aloof with strangers. Very active (perhaps too much so for children), can be nervous, timid. Needs lots of daily outdoor exercise, not for city life.

winning traits: Overall is smart, strong, agile, and graceful; *head* is clean, long, with a smooth forehead, large nose, and a muzzle that is long and deep but not sloppy; *ears* are medium in length, lie close to head, and start about eye level; *legs*, front are straight giving good movement, hind are straight when seen from behind, muscular and set on broad hips; *body* has a deep chest and a straight back that has a slight slope down to tail; *tail* is docked and carried straight out when animal is in motion.

disqualify/penalize: China or wall eyes, nose that is flesh-colored, over/undershot jaw, solid white color or any spot of black, red, orange, lemon, or tan.

considerations: May develop hip dysplasia.
price range: $200–$300.

GERMAN WIREHAIRED POINTER (Sporting)

Very similar to the German Shorthaired Pointer, except for his coat. This is a fine all-around hunting dog. He retrieves from land and water, and works very well as a pointer. His coat will need moderate grooming, and as with most wirehaired breeds, will also need stripping. Sheds lightly if stripped regularly.

coat: Outercoat harsh, wiry, flat, about 1½"–2" long, undercoat dense in winter and thin in summer. *Colors:* liver, liver and white, can be roan, ticked, or spotted.
height/weight: Dog 24"–26", bitch over 22"/55 lbs. average.
behavior: Very similar to that of the German Shorthaired Pointer, but even less adaptable to children as he may be more excitable and restless.
winning traits: Overall a lively, strong animal with a confident sense of himself; *head* is somewhat long and broad with a long, broad, bearded muzzle; *ears* are somewhat round in shape and lie close to head; *legs*, front are straight, hind are muscular and straight when seen from behind; *body* is somewhat long, with a slight slope of the back from withers to tail, the chest is deep, and the loins tight and with a tuck-up; *tail* is docked and carried out and slightly upward.

disqualify/penalize: Any black in coat, flesh-colored nose, coat that is short and smooth, woolly, or excessively long.
considerations: Very prone to getting worms.
price range: $200–$350.

GIANT SCHNAUZER
(Working)

The breed was developed in Germany to drive cattle and is the largest of the three Schnauzer breeds. They are very dependable and gentle with cattle, and can also be used as guard dogs (they have been used extensively to guard breweries in Munich). Expect heavy grooming, stripping, and trimming requiring a professional hand. Sheds little.

coat: Coarse, hard, very thick, double with a wiry outercoat and soft undercoat. *Colors:* solid black or salt and pepper.
height/weight: Dog 25½"–27½", bitch 23½"–25½"/approx. 75 lbs.
behavior: A quick learner, alert and lively, lots of spirit but good, even temperament, fun, devoted. Can be too active for children, can be strong-willed and protective. Needs lots of outdoor exercise.
winning traits: Overall a large dog with a silhouette that is almost square and gives the impression of strength and intel-

ligence; *head* is large and strong with a wide skull, square muzzle, and prominent eyebrows; *ears* are high-set on head, are cropped or natural, when cropped are erect and if left uncropped are button in shape; *legs,* front are strong and straight under high withers, hind are well-muscled and straight when viewed from behind; *body* has a short-coupled, straight back with a strong, deep chest and short loin; *tail* is docked and carried high.

disqualify/penalize: Viciousness, overt shyness, over/undershot jaw, markings not mentioned above.

considerations: May develop hip dysplasia and be prone to dry skin, mange, and epilepsy.

price range: $450 and up.

GOLDEN RETRIEVER
(Sporting)

You will find Golden Retrievers at the top of many obedience contests. They are excellent gun dogs, retrievers, and, more recently, guide dogs for the blind. Their beautiful coat and eagerness to please make them one of the most popular breeds. Expect moderate to heavy grooming and some trimming. Sheds moderately.

coat: Water repellent, thick, straight or wavy, lying flat to body. *Colors:* all shades of golden.

height/weight: Dog 23″–24″/65–75 lbs., bitch 21″–22½″/60–70 lbs.

behavior: A very quick learner, wants to please everyone, loves children. Very obedient and trainable, mild-mannered, gentle, can be timid. Needs a lot of outdoor exercise.

winning traits: Overall has a confident, kind, intelligent expression and is an animal that moves beautifully; *head* is broad and has a straight muzzle and clean lips; *ears* are somewhat short and are set just above eye level; *legs*, front are straight, strong and move freely, hind are well muscled and straight; *body* has a deep chest and a short, somewhat straight loin; *tail* is thick, muscular, and is carried straight or slightly upward and happily.

disqualify/penalize: More than 1-inch deviation from heights mentioned above, under/overshot jaw.

considerations: Normally healthy but may be prone to eye problems, hip dysplasia, allergies, epilepsy.

price range: $350 and up.

GORDON SETTER (Sporting)

This dog was developed in Scotland into one of the top bird dogs. He has a superior nose and the endurance to work with a hunter for long periods. His elegant coat makes him one of the most beautiful of the Setters. Expect to be attentive with grooming and trimming. Sheds moderately.

coat: Straight, shiny, soft, can be slightly wavy but not curly, long on tail, ears, stomach, chest and back of legs. *Colors:* black with tan, chestnut or mahogany markings.

height/weight: Dog 24″–27″/55–80 lbs., bitch 23″–26″/45–70 lbs.

behavior: A quick learner, very good with his family, including children. Gentle, mild-mannered, may be strong-willed, aloof with strangers, may want to roam, needs early training for best results. Needs lots of outdoor exercise.

winning traits: Overall a strong, durable dog with an intelligent alertness; *head* is somewhat heavy but not broad and has a moderately long square muzzle; *ears* are long, close-lying, and set about level with the eyes; *legs*, front are heavy-boned, straight, hind are strong and straight when seen from behind; *body* is short with short, broad loins to the tail; *tail* is natural, medium-long (about to hocks), feathered, and carried straight out.

disqualify/penalize: Predominantly red, tan, or buff animals with markings which are not typical of the Gordon.

considerations: May develop hip dysplasia, allergies, eye problems, epilepsy.
price range: $200–$300.

GREAT DANE (Working)

This dog is not from Denmark but from Germany. He loves children but with his size he may innocently injure them. He was originally used to track and fight wild boar but now is normally a guard dog. Expect moderate grooming and, in spite of his size, light shedding.

coat: Thick, glossy, short and smooth. *Colors:* many are permissible and may include brindle, blue, black, fawn, harlequin.
height/weight: Dog over 30″, bitch over 28″/over 120 lbs.
behavior: May be slow learner, loves everyone, including children. Can be strong-willed, needs consistent and often-repeated hand in training. Needs lots of outdoor exercise, is normally inactive indoors.
winning traits: Overall a giant animal with a smooth, beautifully muscled body and proud bearing; *head* is long, slender, and has a full muzzle and flat skull; *ears* can be uncropped or cropped, if left natural should lie forward and close to head, if cropped should be shaped in proportion to head and held erect; *legs* are long and straight when seen head-on or from rear; *body* is short for the breed's size and has a straight back that slopes

slightly up from the withers, the chest is deep and wide; *tail* is long and hangs straight down when relaxed, out and curved when in motion.

disqualify/penalize: Dogs under minimum height; all-white dogs, merles, solid gray, mouse-gray base with black or white (or both), white with gray spots; harlequins and solid colors on body leaving only white legs, neck, and point of tail; brindle, fawn, blue and black dogs with white forehead line, collar, and belly; docked tails, split noses, narrow or weak chest, protruding sternum.

considerations: One of shortest-lived dogs, prone to hip dysplasia and bloat. Some breeders have bred inferior animals with weak backs and sickly appearance—know your breeder well before buying.

price range: $350–$650.

GREAT PYRENEES (Working)

Fossils of this breed have been found from as far back as the Bronze Age. They were used as sled and cart dogs, protectors of flocks, and watchdogs. So devoted to their job are these animals that they often sacrifice themselves for those they protect. Expect moderate to heavy grooming and shedding.

coat: Impervious to the severest weather, straight, outercoat thick, long, somewhat wavy, undercoat fine. *Colors:* white, or white with gray or tan.

height/weight: Dog 27"–32"/100–125 lbs., bitch 25"–29"/90–115 lbs.

behavior: A somewhat slow learner, one-family dog, good with children. Mild-mannered, may want to roam, can be strong-willed and needs firm, consistent training. Needs lots of outdoor exercise.

winning traits: Overall a huge animal with a lustrous coat and a calm, intelligent bearing; *head* is large and wedge-shaped with a clean muzzle; *ears* are natural, set at about eye level and close to head; *legs* are medium-long, straight, and strong, hind have dewclaws; *body* has a deep brisket, straight back, and broad loins and hips; *tail* is long, bushy, and hangs when relaxed, curls over back when excited.

disqualify/penalize: None.

considerations: Short-lived but normally very healthy, may develop hip dysplasia.

price range: $350 and up.

GREYHOUND (Hound)

There are tomb carvings of this breed dating back to 2900 B.C. in Egypt. Greyhounds were used to hunt deer, foxes, and hare by sight, overtaking them by their speed. Now they are used as popular racing dogs, often clocked at over 40 miles an hour. Expect light grooming and shedding.

coat: Short, smooth. *Colors:* any.

height/weight: Approx. 26"/dog 65–70 lbs., bitch 60–65 lbs.

behavior: A quick learner, good with adults, may be aloof with strangers. Strong-willed, gentle, skittish around sudden noises, quite nervous, needing calm training. Needs lots of outdoor exercise, not suited to city life unless exercised sufficiently.

winning traits: Overall a very strong, agile, streamlined animal; *head* is long and slender but somewhat wide in the skull; *ears* lie back on head and fold against the neck when dog is relaxed; *legs,* front are straight, hind are long and very strong, set on wide hips; *body* has a deep chest and a strong, wide back; *tail* is long and slender and is used as a rudder when running.

disqualify/penalize: None.

considerations: Can be plagued by bloat, sensitive to cold.

price range: $300 and up.

HARRIER (Hound)

Record of these dogs dates back to 400 B.C. As the name implies, they were developed to hunt hare. Their strength and superior nose make them excellent hunters. But for its smaller size the Harrier is almost identical to the English Foxhound. The breed is very rare in the United States. Expect minimal grooming and light shedding.

coat: Smooth, dense, hard, short. *Colors:* most often tri-color (black, tan, and white), or any combination of them.
height/weight: 19″–21″/approx. 45 lbs.
behavior: A quick learner, loves everyone, including children. May be aloof with strangers, may be strong-willed and outgoing, wants to roam. Needs lots of outdoor exercise.
winning traits: Overall is much like the larger English Foxhound or the smaller Beagle, and is a balanced, active animal; *head*, medium-sized; *ears* are high on head and rounded at point; *legs* are straight and well-boned; *body* has a deep chest and a level, strong back; *tail* is carried high (not over back) with a slight curve.
disqualify/penalize: None.
considerations: None, is one of the healthiest breeds.
price range: $125–$300.

IBIZAN (Hound)

This breed orginated in Egypt about five thousand years ago. They have a long, lean, strong look and are spectacular high jumpers. They also have developed into some of the most adaptable hunters, hunting alone or in packs. They are retrievers as well as pointers, and are among the best scent hounds in the world. Expect light grooming and shedding.

coat: Two types—shorthaired is short, smooth, hard; wirehaired is 1″–3″ long, hard, longer on back, thighs, tail. *Colors:* mixtures of red, white, and fawn.

height/weight: Dog 23½″–27½″/approx. 50 lbs., bitch 22½″–26″/42–49 lbs.

behavior: A very quick learner, friendly to everyone, loving in a quiet way, mild-mannered, very good with children. Needs lots of outdoor exercise.

winning traits: Overall a streamlined animal much like a Greyhound, indicating speed and agility; *head* is long, slender, clean of excess flesh, and with very long jaws; *ears* are large, natural, erect, and begin at about eye level; *legs*, front are straight, strong, and light-boned, hind are strong, with sleek muscles and straight bone; *body* has a deep chest and a straight, level, limber back; *tail* is long and low-set.

disqualify/penalize: Colors other than those mentioned above.

considerations: Normally very healthy but may be very sen-

sitive to drugs (insecticides, anesthetics), can experience false pregnancy.
price range: $400–$500.

IRISH SETTER (Sporting)

With their rich, shiny coat and elegant posture, they can be remarkably beautiful. But don't let their elegance fool you; they can be clowns! Speed and good noses make them among the best retrievers, but they are also used as watchdogs. Their life span is unusually long for a large dog. Expect moderate grooming with some trimming. Sheds moderately to heavily.

coat: Moderately long everywhere but on head, forelegs, and tips of ears, where it is short. *Colors:* rich mahogany or chestnut.
height/weight: Dog 27"/70 lbs., bitch 25"/60 lbs.
behavior: A quick learner, loves everyone, including lively children. Gentle, can be strong-willed so needs early training, has truly a free, fun-loving spirit, may want to roam. Needs lots of outdoor exercise, not for city living.
winning traits: Overall an animal with elegant bearing and a movement that is fast and liquid; *head* is long and narrow (about two times as long as it is wide), somewhat domed, and has a square muzzle; *ears* are long, silky, and set below eye level; *legs* are free-moving and straight in front, hind are long and strong

and have good angle in the stifles; *body* is long with a deep chest and a back that slopes slightly downward to tail; *tail* is about the length of the hocks and is carried almost in line with the back.
disqualify/penalize: Crossing or weaving of the legs while in motion, nose which is not black or chocolate.
considerations: May develop hip dysplasia, digestive problems, and heart disease.
price range: $350 and up.

IRISH TERRIER (Terrier)

These dogs make brave guard dogs, and they have been used as messengers as well during wartime. They can be a very lively handful but are perfect for anyone who wants a dog with a sense of humor. Grooming includes stripping and trimming with a professional hand. Sheds lightly.

coat: Outercoat is very thick, harsh, and wiry, undercoat is fine. *Colors:* all red, red wheaten, golden red; puppies may have black hair at birth which disappears as the animal matures.
height/weight: Approx. 18″/dog 27 lbs., bitch 25 lbs.
behavior: A very quick learner, loves his family but is aloof with strangers. Fiery temper, plays roughly, good for adults or older children, start firm-handed training early. Active in and out of doors, needs regular outdoor exercise.
winning traits: Overall an animal that is angular and balanced

in profile and has an eager, agile manner; *head* is long, flat, and somewhat narrow, with strong jaws and with a foreface that is not too strong or short; *ears* are V-shaped, high and folding so the lower edge points toward the eye; *legs* are moderately long, strong, rounded, straight, and well boned, both front and back move straight forward when in motion; *body* is moderately long, straight, and strong, with somewhat arched loins and a deep brisket; *tail* is docked and carried high.

disqualify/penalize: White coloring anywhere, single coat without any undercoat, curly or kinky coat, cowhocks, light-colored eyes, ears that do not prick, nose that is not black, under/overshot jaw, any color not mentioned above, back that is too short.

considerations: None.

price range: $300 and up.

IRISH WATER SPANIEL
(Sporting)

As the name implies, this dog loves the water; he is also a tireless hunter. He has a water-repellent coat, along with two eccentricities: a "rat tail" and a topknot that peaks between the eyes. Expect quite a lot of grooming and trimming, which may require a professional hand. Sheds little.

coat: Covered with ringlets of various lengths all over body except on tail. *Color:* solid liver.

height/weight: Dog 22"–24"/55–65 lbs., bitch 22"–23"/45–58 lbs.

behavior: A very quick learner, truly a dog for one special person but likes his family. Good with older children, can be strong-willed and shy. Needs lots of outdoor exercise.

winning traits: Overall an alert, outgoing dog with a strong build and good movement; *head* is somewhat large and high-domed with a square muzzle; *ears* are long and low-set, with tight curls everywhere but on the feathered ends; *legs,* front are straight and medium-long with large feet, hind are moderately long and set on round, wide hips; *body* has a back that slopes upward slightly to the tail, and has short loins that are strong and wide; *tail* is called a rat tail, as it tapers to a point and has short hair, its length does not extend to the hocks.

disqualify/penalize: White on the chest.

considerations: May develop hip dysplasia and be prone to ear infections, may drool.

price range: $200–$300.

IRISH WOLFHOUND (Hound)

Their size, scruffy coat, and piercing eyes make this breed look intimidating, but under that exterior is the gentlest of souls and one of the best companions. In the past they were trained to hunt wolves and kill them by catching them and shaking them by the neck. Expect moderate grooming and stripping. Sheds little.

coat: Rough, hard, wiry. *Colors:* white, gray, fawn, brindle, red, black.

height/weight: (Minimum) dog 32″/120 lbs., bitch 30″/105 lbs.

behavior: A quick learner, is very good with everyone, loves children, gentle, kind, patient. Somewhat inactive indoors, but needs lots of outdoor exercise.

winning traits: Overall a huge, scruffy animal with lines of great power and speed; *head* is long and medium-wide, the muzzle long and somewhat pointed; *ears* are small and carried back along neck when animal is relaxed; *legs* are long and muscular, and straight when viewed from front or back; *body* has a very wide, deep chest and a long, wide back with arched loins; *tail* is long and somewhat curved.

disqualify/penalize: Head too heavy or light, long ears that hang flat to face, short neck, dewlap, chest too narrow or too broad, back too sunken or too straight, front legs that are bent, overbent fetlocks, feet that are twisted or that have spread toes, tail that curls too much, too light muscle, short body, lips or nose that are liver-colored or without pigment.

considerations: Generally short-lived, may bloat, develop hip dysplasia, and be very sensitive to anesthetics.
price range: $500–$700.

ITALIAN GREYHOUND
(Toy)

A small version of the Greyhound, this elegant breed has been known for more than two thousand years. Slight but not fragile, affectionate and fastidious, it has been a very aristocratic pet throughout history. Expect little grooming and light shedding.

coat: Short, thin, glossy, satiny. *Colors:* any colors or markings except tan.
height/weight: 13″–15″/8 lbs. average
behavior: A very quick learner, normally shy, gentle, obeys readily, can be aloof with strangers, is definitely a one-family dog. Best to train early to reduce tendency toward shyness, not suited to busy, noisy households. Needs little exercise.
winning traits: Overall a fragile-looking animal with a high-stepping movement; *head* is slender and long with a long, fine muzzle; *ears* are small and carried back when animal is relaxed, carried out from the head and to the side when animal is alert; *legs* are fine, long, and straight, with well-muscled thighs; *body* is medium-long, with an arched back and tucked-up flanks; *tail* is long, slender, low-set, and curved at the end.

disqualify/penalize: Brindle markings, tan markings resembling those found on black and tan dogs of other breeds.
considerations: Bones break easily, is bothered by cold.
price range: $200 and up.

JAPANESE CHIN (Toy)

This breed is also called the Japanese Spaniel. They are intelligent and look it with their high-prancing walk and luxurious coat. They can be tough as well as gentle, and rarely forget a friend or an enemy. They are very adaptable and can live in most climates and in almost any environment. Expect somewhat attentive grooming and moderate shedding

coat: Long, straight, fluffy, thick. *Colors:* white with black, lemon, or red, nose must blend with coat color.
height/weight: 9"/two weights—7 lbs. and under; over 7 lbs.
behavior: A quick learner, very alert, mild-mannered, playful, likes everyone but size limits his being with young children Can be lively indoors, but needs little outdoor exercise.
winning traits: Overall a high-stepping animal with a compact body and a self-confident demeanor; *head* is large, wide, and rounded, with a very short muzzle; *ears,* small and V-shaped, are high-set and wide on head; *legs* are small-boned; *body* is compact, almost square, with a wide brisket; *tail* is carried over back (but is not ringed)

disqualify/penalize: In black and white dogs, a nose that is any color but black.
considerations: Prone to eye problems, wheezing and breathing problems, may be bothered by heat.
price range: $150–$250.

KEESHOND (Nonsporting)

This breed (plural, *Keeshonden*) has no desire to hunt and no true specialized use except that of watchdog. He is the national dog of Holland, and served as companion on barges that worked the Rhine River. Some experts believe that he is an ancestor of the Pomeranian, despite their size difference. Expect heavy shedding twice a year, moderate grooming and shedding for balance of year.

coat: Extremely thick, long, straight, lionlike around the neck, trouserlike on the hind legs and rump, thick undercoat. *Colors:* mixtures of gray and black.
height/weight: Dog 18″, bitch 17″/40 lbs. average.
behavior: A quick learner, good with everyone, especially children, gentle, can be strong-willed. Needs a moderate amount of outdoor exercise.
winning traits: Overall a short-coupled animal with a foxy, intelligent expression; *head* is wedge-shaped, with a pleasing mask and a muzzle that is well balanced with the rest of the

head; *ears* are small, V-shaped, and high-set on head; *legs* are well boned, cream-colored, and straight, with feathering on the thighs; *body* is compact with a straight back that slopes gently upward from the tail, a deep chest and a tucked-up stomach; *tail* is long, high-set, and curled tightly over the back.

disqualify/penalize: Absence of "spectacles" in facemask, over/undershot jaw, apple head or absence of stop, ears not erect when at attention, white foot or feet, tail not lying close to back or not carried over back when moving, coat that is silky, wavy, curly, or parted down back, any solid-colored dog.

considerations: None.

price range: $300 and up.

KERRY BLUE TERRIER
(Terrier)

He is so scrappy that he will fight to the death in battle but is also loving and very intelligent. He delights in hunting small game, and is both a land and a water retriever as well as an excellent herder. In the United States, show competition requires careful grooming to strict standards. Expect heavy grooming and professional trimming. Sheds little.

coat: Thick, wavy, soft. *Colors:* any shade of blue or gray.

height/weight: 18″–19½″, bitch 17½″–19″/33–40 lbs.

behavior: A quick learner, is loyal to one family, and is aloof with strangers. May bark a lot, can be stubborn, willful, strong, needs sometimes forceful training, should be introduced to people as early as possible for best results. Needs lots of outdoor exercise.

winning traits: Overall an angular animal with good proportions and an outgoing, friendly demeanor; *head* is long, flat, and moderately wide; *ears* are V-shaped and small, and fold just above the top of the skull; *legs* are somewhat long, well-muscled and strong, moving straight forward when in motion; *body* has a short back, deep chest, and a short, strong loin; *tail* is docked and carried high.

disqualify/penalize: Hind legs with dewclaws, totally black color.

considerations: Normally has very strong health, may have eye (tear) problems.
price range: $325 and up.

KOMONDOR (Working)

This breed (plural, *Komon dorok*) is characteristically very courageous, and may be the best sheep guard dog in the world Their outstanding coat is thick, usually falling in mat ted tags, and it is heavy enough to protect them from weather and most attackers. Expect lots of bathing with long drying ses sions, and little shedding.

coat: Long, shaggy, woolly, thick, usually unkempt. *Colors:* white.
height/weight: Dog at least 25½", bitch 23½"/90 lbs. average.
behavior: May be a slow learner, dog for one family, aloof with strangers. Stubborn but easygoing, playful, can be too protec tive, headstrong unless trained at early age. Active indoors, also needs lots of outdoor exercise
winning traits: Overall a muscular animal that has a rectan gular body and shows great energy; *head* is short and broad with a straight muzzle and domed skull; *ears* are V-shaped and hang; *legs*, front are straight and muscular, hind are well-boned and muscled, and straight when seen from behind, dewclaws are removed; *body* is deep and wide with a straight back; *tail* is long and slightly curved.

disqualify/penalize: Any color but white, coat that is un
corded by the time animal is two years old, hair that is short or
smooth on head and legs, light-colored eyes, pink nose, under/
overshot jaw, ears that are erect (or are nearly erect), dewlaps
on neck, substandard size
considerations: May develop hip dysplasia.
price range: $350–$500.

KUVASZ (Working)

This dog (plural, *Kuvaszok*)
seems to form a fast impression
of anyone he meets, and never
to forget it. He was bred to be
an excellent farm dog, and is an
outstanding guard. His origins
are probably in Tibet, but ulti-
mately he traveled to Hungary,
where he became the breed
type we know today. Expect
moderate grooming and shedding.

coat: Double, long, thick, wavy everywhere but on head and
front of legs, where it is short. *Colors:* white.
height/weight: Dog 28″–29½″/100–120 lbs., bitch 26″–
27½″/75–95 lbs.
behavior: A quick learner, can be aloof, even with his family,
but very loyal and protective, suspects all strangers. Stubborn,
needs firm, knowledgeable hand in training. Seems always
active, needs a lot of outdoor exercise.

winning traits: Overall a very large animal with proud bearing and apparent strength and stamina; *head* is long and of medium width, with a clean muzzle with no excess skin; *ears* are V-shaped and somewhat rounded, inner edge touching the cheek and outer edge standing away from the head; *legs*, front are straight and well muscled, hind are long and strong under wide hips; *body* has a deep chest protruding somewhat to front and a moderately long, straight back with short, strong loins; *tail* is long (to hocks), slightly curved, and hangs low.

disqualify/penalize: Over/undershot jaw, animals more than 2 inches below size standard, any color but white.

considerations: May develop hip dysplasia.

price range: $300 and up.

LABRADOR RETRIEVER
(Sporting)

This is the most popular of all retrievers in the United States. Reliable, strong, sensible, and obedient as a hunting companion, he is also a good herding dog, guard dog, and guide dog for the blind. He comes not from Labrador but from Newfoundland. Expect moderate grooming and shedding.

coat: Short, very thick, and straight. *Colors:* black, yellow or chocolate (on chocolates, a small white patch on chest is permissible).

height/weight: Dog 22½″–24½″, bitch 21½″–23½″/60 lbs. average.

behavior: A very quick learner, loves everyone, especially children. Obedient, easily trained, gentle. Needs lots of outdoor exercise but is willing to forego activity when in harness as a guide dog.

winning traits: Overall appears intelligent, active, and strong, with a lustrous, short coat; *head* is wide, with a wide nose and clean lips; *ears* are hanging, low-set, and placed back on head; *legs*, front are straight, giving good movement and are medium-long, hind are well muscled and straight when seen from behind; *body* has a deep, wide chest and is well proportioned but strong; *tail* is about to hocks, strong and thick and is carried out and alert.

disqualify/penalize: Feathers in coat, tail that curls over back, wavy or soft coat, pink nose.

considerations: May develop hip dysplasia, allergies, and eye problems.
price range: $250–$500.

LAKELAND TERRIER
(Terrier)

This is one of the oldest of the Terrier breeds. Originally he was known as the Patterdale Terrier and was used to hunt foxes, badgers, and otters. Now his gay, self-confident ways make him a wonderful pet for those who do not mind being attentive to his daily needs for grooming, trimming, and stripping.

coat: Double, outercoat is hard and wiry, undercoat is soft. *Colors:* red, grizzle, blue, wheaten, black, liver; and black, blue, or grizzle with tan.
height/weight: 14″–15″/approx. 17 lbs.
behavior: A quick learner, friendly with everyone but loyal to his family. Outgoing, feisty, can be stubborn and hard to housebreak. Very lively in and out of doors, needs some outdoor exercise.
winning traits: Overall angular in profile, with a square build and a graceful, confident demeanor; *head* is rectangular and flat, with a moderately wide skull, broad muzzle, and straight nose; *ears* are V-shaped, and fold just above the top of the skull; *legs*

are strong and well boned, straight when viewed from front or back; *body* is almost square, with a deep chest and straight back; *tail* is docked and carried high.

disqualify/penalize: Over/undershot jaw, dewclaws, tail that curls over back, paddlefoot or gait that toes in, shyness.

considerations: Normally healthy, but dry skin may pose discomfort.

price range: Approximately $300.

LHASA APSO (Nonsporting)

This dog, originally from Tibet, can withstand that country's extremes of weather. Despite their small size, they were used as inside guard dogs, trained to warn of intruders. They are now primarily companion dogs for those owners who enjoy grooming a very long coat. Expect moderate shedding.

coat: Thick, very long, straight. *Colors:* shades of blond, gold, gray, black, white, or brown, and may include darker beard and tips of ears.

height/weight: Dog 10″–11″, bitch 9″–10″/approx. 15 lbs.

behavior: A quick learner, loyal to his family but aloof with strangers. Outgoing and lively, can have a quick temper and be stubborn, best living with adults or older children. Very active in and out of doors, requires moderate outdoor exercise.

winning traits: Overall small, long, and low-set, and carrying itself gaily; *head* is narrow and somewhat flat, with medium-length muzzle and slightly undershot jaw; *ears* hang and are covered with long hair; *body* is long, and strong in loin; *tail* is natural and carried high over back, may be kinked or screwed.

disqualify/penalize: Light-colored eyes, muzzle that is square, low-set tail.

considerations: May have kidney problems, allergies, and eye problems.

price range: $300–$500.

MALTESE (Toy)

The breed originated in Malta as far back as 384 B.C. They have been pets of royalty and the wealthy throughout their long history. Though classified as Toys, they are actually spaniels. Expect a lot of daily combing, and regular bathing. Sheds little.

coat: Single, very long, silky, straight. *Colors:* pure white is preferred, lemon or light tan on ears is permitted but is less desirable than white.

height/weight: 5″/approx. 4–6 lbs.

behavior: A quick learner, loyal to one family, normally aloof with strangers. Outgoing, lively, obedient, gentle-mannered, eager and fun-loving, best with adults and older children. Very active.

winning traits: Overall a small animal with elegant long hair and a short body; *head* is medium-long and moderately rounded, with a medium-length tapered muzzle; *ears* are set low on head and are covered with long hair; *legs* are fine, front are straight, hind are strong with small feet; *body* is compact and has a straight back, deep chest, and a tight, strong loin; *tail* is long, lying over back.

disqualify/penalize: Coat that is kinky (even slightly), woolly, or curly, legs that toe in or out, cowhocks.

considerations: May have problems with teeth, skin, and eyes, may be prone to respiratory troubles, slipped stifle.

price range: $300 and up.

MANCHESTER TERRIER
(Standard-size Terrier, and the smaller-size Toy)

Originating in nineteenth-century England as a cross between a Whippet bitch and a dog of unknown origin, the Manchester has a sleek, elegant look. Both varieties make excellent companion pets. The breed is not prone to the normal dog odors, it requires very light grooming, and shedding is light.

coat: Short, thick, close, shiny. *Colors:* black with rich mahogany markings.

height/weight: Two varieties—Standard, 14″–16″/12–22 lbs.; Toy, less than 12 lbs.

behavior: A quick learner, devoted to his family but may be aloof with strangers. Very active and alert, can be stubborn and outgoing, good for adults. The Toy variety may be somewhat overnervous.

winning traits: Overall has a smooth, graceful outline and an aristocratic bearing; *head* is slender and long, with an almost flat skull; *ears* on Toys are close-set, erect and pointed, on Standard variety are also close-set and either cropped and carried erect or uncropped and button or erect; *legs* are straight when seen from front or back view; *body* is somewhat short and has a deep, narrow chest; *tail* is moderately short and is carried low (not higher than the back).

disqualify/penalize: Dogs that weigh over 22 pounds, colors other than those above, in the Toy variety ears that are cropped or cut.

considerations: Can be troubled by cold, skin problems; Toys can develop slipped stifle and be prone to fractures.

price range: Standard $250–$350; Toy $150–$200.

MASTIFF (Working)

This dog is a giant, but very gentle in spite of its size, and one of the best family dogs. The breed has existed for over two thousand years. During its long history it has been used as a watchdog and a fighting dog, often accompanying soldiers in wartime. Expect moderate grooming and shedding.

coat: Outercoat is coarse and short, undercoat thick and short. *Colors:* apricot, or shades of fawn with dark muzzle, ears, and nose.

height/weight: Dog minimum 30″, bitch 27½″/approx. 185 lbs.

behavior: May be a slow learner but is trainable with steady, patient work, loves everyone, including lively children. Very gentle, patient, mild-mannered, may be stubborn. Inactive indoors, but needs lots of outdoor exercise.

winning traits: Overall a massive animal with a compact, well-balanced look; *head* is very large, wide, and muscular with a moderately rounded skull and a short, broad nose with generous flews; *ears* are disproportionately small, are V-shaped and hang close to face when dog is relaxed; *legs* are set wide, straight and muscular front and back; *body* is wide and has a straight back and muscular loins; *tail* is natural, long and curved.

disqualify/penalize: Excess skin on neck and shoulders, high-cut flank, tail carried over the back.

considerations: Has a short lifespan, may snore or have trouble breathing, may develop hip dysplasia.

price range: $550 and up.

MINIATURE PINSCHER
(Toy)

This small dog has so much poise and self-assurance that he seems bigger than he really is. He also has a wonderfully intelligent look, with a high carriage to his tail and the high-stepping gait of a hackney pony. He has been popular for many centuries in Germany and Scandinavia. Expect light grooming and shedding.

coat: Short, smooth, sleek, straight, close. *Colors:* black with rust-red markings, solid red/brown/chocolate with rust or yellow markings.

height/weight: 10″–12½″/approx. 8 lbs.

behavior: A quick learner, likes his family but is best with somewhat adult children. Gutsy, very alert, can be stubborn and nervous, may bark a lot. Very active but does not need much outdoor exercise.

winning traits: Overall a square animal with a balanced, compact profile and a proud hackney-gaited movement; *head* is flat and proportioned to the body, with a strong muzzle; *ears* are erect and high-set on head; *legs* are strong and straight from front and back views, thighs are muscular, and there should be no dewclaws on the hind legs; *body* is compact and has a straight back that slopes slightly downward from the shoulders, with a deep chest; *tail* is docked and is carried high.

disqualify/penalize: Any color but those mentioned above, more than ½″ of white on any part of body, sizes above or below standard.

considerations: Probably the hardiest Toy, but may be bothered by cold and dislocated joints.

price range: $250 and up.

MINIATURE SCHNAUZER
(Terrier)

Their origins stem from the Affenpinscher, the Poodle, and the small Standard Schnauzer. They were bred in Germany, where they hunted and killed rats. Though small, they have the same outgoing, bold way typical of Terriers. They are some of the most adaptable dogs for small city houses and apartments. Daily grooming, with a professional hand trimming and stripping. Expect little shedding.

coat: Wiry, hard, and with a close undercoat. *Colors:* black, salt and pepper, black and silver.

height/weight: 12"–14"/approx. 15 lbs.

behavior: A very quick learner, likes his family but may be aloof with strangers, good with children who are not too rough. Very alert, may bark a lot. Very active indoors and out, needs some outdoor exercise. (Puppy mills have bred some inferior animals; know your breeder before buying.)

winning traits: Overall a smart-looking, hardy animal with a robust, intelligent demeanor; *head* is flat with a moderately long and blunt muzzle; *ears* set high on head and either cropped and erect or natural and V-shaped, with a fold close to the skull; *legs* are straight when seen from front or rear, and front have tight-fitting elbows; *body* is short, with a deep chest and flank; *tail* is docked and carried merrily.

disqualify/penalize: Over/undershot mouth, cowhocks, or bowed back legs, low-set tail, gait that is not straight and strong.

considerations: May develop cataracts, have problems with kidneys, and become affected with Von Willebrands's disease.

price range: $250 and up.

NEWFOUNDLAND (Working)

If you like very large dogs, this one is almost ideal. Intelligent and easily trained, they are extremely strong, and are natural guards. They love water, are excellent swimmers, and they are among the best companions and friends. Expect moderate grooming and heavy shedding.

coat: Thick, oily, coarse. *Colors:* usually black, but also can be tinged with bronze or black with white on feet, chest, rump, and tail.

height/weight: Dog 28″/150 lbs, bitch 26″/120 lbs.

behavior: A quick learner, loving and gentle with everyone and exceptional with children. Kind, will guard and protect its family but is careless about protecting property. Needs lots of outdoor exercise but does not necessarily need to run.

winning traits: Overall a balanced, square-looking animal with a beautiful coat and proud bearing; *head* is huge, broad with a broad, deep muzzle; *ears* are small, triangular, and set back on head; *legs* are broad-set, muscled well, and heavily boned; *body* is wide and has a deep chest and straight back; *tail* is natural and long and has a slight curve.

disqualify/penalize: Colors other than those above.

considerations: Short-lived, may slobber, is bothered by heat and allergies, may develop hip dysplasia.

price range: $350 and up.

NORFOLK TERRIER (Terrier)

This is basically the same animal as the Norwich Terrier but with button ears. In the United States in the 1920s, this breed (along with Norwich Terriers) was known as the Jones Terrier. They are spirited and lively, as are most Terriers, and though small they are actually a sporting type. Expect moderate grooming, stripping and trimming, light shedding.

coat: Lies close, straight, wiry, with an undercoat, coat more abundant around shoulders and neck, and should look natural even for show. *Colors:* grizzle, tan, black-and-tan, red, wheaten.

height/weight: 10"/approx. 12 lbs.

behavior: Quick learner, loves everyone. Outgoing, lively and alert, can be stubborn, may bark a lot. Needs moderate outdoor exercise.

winning traits: Overall a small, sturdy, compact animal; *head* is broad, strong, and short, with a skull that is somewhat rounded; *ears* are V-shaped and fold at the top of the skull line; *legs* are short, powerful, set on wide hips, with muscular thighs; *body* is moderately long with a straight back, deep chest, and strong loins; *tail* is docked short and carried high.

disqualify/penalize: White markings in coat, coat that appears too tidy, animals not in top physical condition.

considerations: May be prone to skin allergies.

price range: $250 and up.

NORWEGIAN ELKHOUND
(Hound)

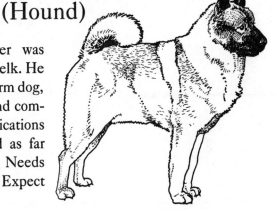

This wonderful hunter was used in Norway to hunt elk. He is also often used as a farm dog, sled dog, guard dog, and companion. There are indications that the breed existed as far back as the Stone Age. Needs moderate grooming. Expect heavy shedding.

coat: Outercoat somewhat harsh, long, straight, very thick, undercoat soft. *Colors:* gray with black tips on each hair, lighter colors on chest, stomach, and legs.

height/weight: Dog 20½″, bitch 19¼″/approx. 50 lbs.

behavior: A quick learner, likes everyone including children. Normally easygoing but can be headstrong and should be trained early with a firm hand, can be nervous and bark a lot. Needs some outdoor exercise but can adapt to city living.

winning traits: Overall a proud, alert animal that is short-coupled and strong; *head* is wide with a tapering muzzle; *ears* are erect, pointed, and high-set on head; *legs*, front are medium-boned and straight, hind are on broad hips and are straight when seen from behind; *body* is square and short-coupled with a deep, broad chest and a straight back; *tail* is curled over the back.

disqualify/penalize: Colors other than mentioned above.

considerations: Cysts are common, may develop hip dysplasia and eye problems.

price range: $300 and up.

NORWICH TERRIER (Terrier)

When they were brought to the United States after World War I, these dogs (along with the Norfolk Terriers) were known as Jones Terriers. Even though they are short, they are fast enough to accompany mounted horsemen. Although good house pets, they may not adjust well to being sendentary. Expect moderate to heavy grooming, including some trimming and stripping, and little shedding.

coat: Close, hard, wiry with an undercoat. *Colors:* red, black, tan, grizzle, and wheaten.

height/weight: 10″/11–12 lbs.

behavior: A very quick learner, loves everyone, including lively children. Quite stubborn, fun, has lots of spirit, may bark a lot. Extremely active in/outdoors, needs lots of outdoor exercise.

winning traits: Overall a short, compact animal with a bright and friendly outlook; *head* is wide with a short muzzle and a moderately domed skull; *ears* are wide-set on head and pointedly erect; *legs* are short, powerful, and straight when seen from front and back, the thighs are muscular and the hips broad; *body* is somewhat short and deep with a straight back; *tail* is docked short, and carried high.

disqualify/penalize: Coats too trimmed and clipped before show (should appear as natural as possible), white in coat, animal that does not appear hardy and fit.

considerations: Can have allergies.
price range: $250 and up.

OLD ENGLISH SHEEPDOG
(Herding)

These dogs were bred to guard sheep and drive them to market, but are adaptable enough to be trained easily as retrievers and as sled dogs. Their easy, ambling gait is deceptive, for they are among the strongest and best-muscled dogs. Expect heavy grooming and light trimming, moderate shedding.

coat: Lots of hair, hard, shaggy. *Colors:* gray, grizzle, blue, and any combination with or without white.
height/weight: At least 22″/approx. 95 lbs.
behavior: May be a slow learner, affectionate, likes everyone, including children. May be stubborn but trainable. (Puppy mills have bred inferior animals that can be nervous, unpredictable with all, and difficult to train.) Needs lots of outdoor exercise.
winning traits: Overall a strong, short-coupled dog that is very well balanced and has a beautiful flowing movement; *head* is full with a square jaw; *ears* are somewhat small and lie flat to sides of head; *legs*, front are straight with strong bone, the hind are well muscled; *body* is short with a deep, full chest; *tail* is natural and very short.

disqualify/penalize: Tail longer than 1½"–2" in grown dogs, colors of fawn or brown.
considerations: May drool, may develop hip dysplasia, eye problems.
price range: $400–$600.

OTTER HOUND (Hound)

They are excellent swimmers, with webbed feet and strong tails, and their noses are superb for hunting. As their name suggests, they were developed to hunt otters and have never gained broad popularity in the United States. The breed is accepted now primarily for their novelty. Expect moderate grooming and shedding.

coat: Hard, thick, almost waterproof. *Colors:* any color is permissible.
height/weight: Dog 24"–27"/75–115 lbs., bitch 22"–26"/65–100 lbs.
behavior: May learn slowly, gentle and loving with everyone, including children. Mild-mannered, can be stubborn, responds to training with a calm, consistent hand. Needs a lot of outdoor exercise.
winning traits: Overall a large, strong, square animal with a rough coat; *head* is covered with long hair and the structure is large but narrow with a long, narrow, square jaw; *ears* are long,

low-set, and hang close to head; *legs*, front are straight and large-boned, hind are straight when seen from behind and are well muscled with large webbed feet; *body* has a deep chest, straight back; *tail* is natural, long, curved and carried high when in motion.

disqualify/penalize: Over/undershot jaw, animals lacking an undercoat, outercoat which is soft or longer than 6 inches, nose that is any color but black or liver.

considerations: Normally very healthy but tends to snore, may develop hip dysplasia (though rare for a dog of this size), often has digestive problems, including gas, prone to hemophilia.

price range: $300 and up.

PAPILLON (Toy)

This breed was developed in Italy but took its name from the French word for butterfly, which describes the look of the ears when they are erect. The Papillon is one of the best house pets, and often takes top honors in the obedience ring. The long coat needs moderate grooming and light trimming. Sheds moderately.

coat: Long, silky, flowing, straight, no undercoat. *Colors:* white with any color markings except liver, head markings should be symmetrical.

height/weight: 8″–11″/4–7 lbs

behavior: A quick learner, loving and gentle with everyone but because of its size should be with children who are not too rough. May be nervous and somewhat highstrung. Active indoors and needs only occasional outside exercise.

winning traits: Overall a small, fine animal with butterfly ears and lively disposition; *head* is small and medium-wide with a fine, short muzzle; *ears* are either erect and resemble butterfly wings, or are drop ears; *legs* are fine-boned, slender, and have good movement, front and back are straight when viewed from behind; *body* is somewhat long and has a straight, level back, medium-deep chest, and a tucked-up stomach; *tail* is long and carried high over back.

disqualify/penalize: Ears that are too small, too high, pointed, only partly up or set such that only one ear is up, short tail or one that is too low or does not arch up over back, stiff hip movement, nose any color but black, coat that is all white or that has no white in it, sway or roach back.

considerations: Bothered by cold, fractures, and slipped stifle.

price range: $200–$300.

PEKINGESE (Toy)

The Pekingese was the Sacred Lion Dog of China. A nickname was also the "sleeve dog" because he was small enough to carry around in one. In spite of their size, they are strong and, unlike many of the Toys, have great stamina. Expect attentive grooming and moderate shedding

coat: Long, flat, straight, heavy on legs, tail, toes, and mane. *Colors:* any allowable, with preference to black muzzle and black around eyes.

height/weight: Approx. 6"/maximum 14 lbs.

behavior: A very quick learner, loves his family, good with older children, may be aloof with strangers. Somewhat inactive indoors, may bark a lot. Needs minimal exercise.

winning traits: Overall an animal that looks like a tiny lion with full mane and a strong, brave demeanor; *head* is very large, wide and flat with a very short, wrinkled muzzle; *ears* are long and shaped like hearts; *legs*, front are short, bowed, and have flat, turned-out feet; *body* is broad and heavy in front and is proportionately deep with a straight back; *tail* is long and set high over back.

disqualify/penalize: Overshot mouth, bulging eyes, or lower jaw not lining up with upper jaw.

considerations: Prone to breathing, back, and eye problems, bothered by heat.

price range: $350 and up.

PHARAOH HOUND (Hound)

This lovely, lean dog is a member of the Greyhound family and originated in Egypt over five thousand years ago. There are references to the breed in art from the tomb of Tutankhamen. They are fast enough to have hunted gazelles, and they have a truly elegant beauty. Need light grooming and shed little.

coat: Short, shiny, can be soft or somewhat harsh. *Colors:* tan or chestnut with white on tail tip, chest, toes, and nose.

height/weight: Dog 23″–25″/bitch 21″–24″.

behavior: A quick learner in a quiet way, loves everyone, including children. Mild-mannered, can be strong-willed, may bark a lot. Needs lots of outdoor exercise.

winning traits: Overall an animal that is sleek, graceful, and fast with a liquid movement; *head* is long and narrow with apparent bones; *ears* are wide at root, long, and erect; *legs*, front are strong, trim, and straight, hind are strong and well muscled; *body* has a deep chest and a moderately long back that slopes downward slightly to tail; *tail* is curved, long (to hocks or below), tapered, and carried high when the dog is in motion.

disqualify/penalize: Nose any color but flesh-colored, corkscrew tail, white color on coat other than as described above, movement that throws feet sideways or looks like a hackney gait, flecked coloration.

considerations: Normally healthy but may have hip dysplasia, blood disorders, and heart problems.

price range: $400–$500.

POINTER (Sporting)

Pointers originated in Spain but were developed in England. They were bred originally to find hare in field hunts, and they develop their hunting skills very early. An athletic breed with lots of energy, stamina, and speed, they are intelligent enough to be able to work with handlers they do not know. Expect light grooming and moderate shedding.

coat: Short, hard, flat. *Colors.* liver, orange, lemon, black, either solid or mixed with white

height/weight: Dog 25"–28"/55–75 lbs., bitch 23"–26"/45–65 lbs.

behavior: May be a slow learner. Loving and gentle with everyone, including children, if raised with a family beginning in early life; if not with a family early enough he may become timid and aloof. Needs lots of outdoor exercise.

winning traits: Overall is powerful and agile, with proud, intelligent carriage; *head* is medium-wide with a muzzle that is moderately long, deep, and tidy, eyes are round; *ears* are set at eye-level and hang, coming to points; *legs*, front are straight, hind are muscular and give good movement; *body* has a deep chest and a tuck up in the loins; *tail* is natural (not docked), can be down to the hocks, and is carried out or slightly up.

disqualify/penalize: Timidity, light-colored eyes, tail that is docked or longer than hocks, or is carried between legs, high, prancing gait

considerations: May develop hip dysplasia, is prone to cysts.
price range: $250 and up.

POMERANIAN (Toy)

In spite of their size, this breed may have descended from the sled dogs of Iceland. They are members of the Spitz family. Almost a century ago, when the breed started becoming popu lar, they were much larger ani mals, weighing as much as thirty pounds. Expect moder ate grooming and light trim ming on its beautiful coat. Sheds heavily

coat: Two coats, undercoat soft and fluffy, outercoat thick, long, straight, shiny, with a very thick frill around the neck. *Colors:* solid or varied shades in any color, parti-color of white with any other evenly distributed color.
height/weight: 7"/3–7 lbs.
behavior: A very quick learner, very good with its adult family, aloof with strangers. Extremely active, knows everything that goes on around it, may be stubborn but very obedient with a trainer whose will is stronger than its own. Happy staying indoors.
winning traits: Overall a tiny animal with a short body and an alert, intelligent manner; *head* looks foxy, with a small delicate muzzle and a wedge-shape (not domed); *ears* are set high on

head and are erect; *legs* are medium-long and straight when seen from front or hind view; *body* is short, with a straight back and deep chest; *tail* is carried high and flat over back.

disqualify/penalize: Light-colored eye rims and nose, under shot jaw, elbows that stand out, cowhocks, coat that lies too flat or is too soft, a dog of one "whole" color with white on feet, legs, or chest, too much trimming of coat before show.

considerations: May develop teeth or gum problems, eye or tear difficulties, heart disease, may be prone to epilepsy.

price range: About $300.

POODLE (Nonsporting)

Though this is the national dog of France, the breed was most likely developed in Germany. It may be the most intelligent of all canines, often seeming more human than dog. Poodles have been used in many ways: as water retrievers, herders, guards, and performers. All three varieties are very much alike, except in size. Expect lots of grooming and professional trimming. Sheds little.

STANDARD POODLE

coat: Thick, harsh, corded when not groomed, woolly when groomed. *Colors:* blue, gray, silver, brown, cream, or apricot.

height/weight: Standard over 15″, Miniature 10″–15″, Toy under 10″.

behavior: An extremely quick learner, very good with its family, including children (except for the Toy and Miniature which may be too highstrung for children). All are gentle, loving, and charming. Standard is somewhat quiet indoors; Miniature and Toy are very active indoors and out.

winning traits: Overall a square-built animal with elegant carriage and intelligent demeanor; *head* is somewhat rounded and long, with a slender muzzle; *ears* are hanging, long and somewhat wide; *legs* are strong and straight when seen from front or back, feet turn neither in nor out; *body* is as high at the shoulders as it is long from the chest to the rump (square), with a deep chest, straight back, and strong, wide loin; *tail* is docked moderately long and carried high.

disqualify/penalize: Coat that is not clipped correctly, parti-colored animals, animals that are over or under standard sizes.

considerations: Prone to eye and ear problems, gas, hip dysplasia.

price range: $300 and up.

TOY POODLE

PORTUGUESE WATER DOG
(Working)

With its water-repellent coat and webbed feet, this is truly a dog bred for water. In Portugal, it was developed to retrieve fish that escaped nets and to recover nets that were broken or separated from boats. Its coat is one that tends to be inoffensive to allergy sufferers. Expect moderate grooming and heavy trimming requiring a professional hand. Sheds little.

coat: Thick, heavy, either wavy or curly, clipped either in a lion clip (shaved over the rear half but left longer at the tip of the tail) or clipped in the working clip (left no longer than 1 inch all over the body except on the tip of the tail, where it is left long). *Colors:* black, brown, or white (can be in combination with each other).

height/weight: Dog 20″–23″/42–60 lbs., bitch 17″–21″/35–50 lbs.

behavior: A very quick learner, very loving with its family and children. Protective, gentle (except to intruders), loves to eat, very intelligent and easily trained. Needs lots of outdoor exercise.

winning traits: Overall a medium-sized, strong, and balanced animal; *head* is broad with a high forehead and strong, clean muzzle; *legs* are well muscled with strongly muscled thighs for speed and without dewclaws, straight when seen from front or rear; *body* has a wide, deep chest with a short neck and nice tuck-up; *tail* is natural, strong, and held over back when attentive.

disqualify/penalize: Any fault that hinders the working ability of the animal.

considerations: May develop hip dysplasia.

price range: $450–$800.

PUG (Toy)

History of this breed predates 400 B.C. It probably originated in China but has become very popular in Holland and France over the last two centuries. It is truly an adaptable little fellow and is happy in a country or city setting. They need very little grooming and shed little as well.

coat: Soft, short, glossy, fine. *Colors:* body is silver, apricot, fawn, or black with black mask.

height/weight: Not over 12″/14–18 lbs.

behavior: A quick learner, loves his family and is very happy with children, may be aloof with strangers. Gentle, may be stubborn, has a stable temperament. Needs only a little outdoor exercise.

winning traits: Overall a very square, short-coupled animal; *head* is very large in proportion to the body, with a short pushed-in muzzle; *ears* are small, and button or rose-shaped; *legs* are moderately long, straight, and muscular; *body* is short, wide, and strong; *tail* is tightly curved over hip (a double curl is highly desirable).

disqualify/penalize: Apple head, coat that is woolly.

considerations: Prone to breathing difficulties and eye problems.

price range: $250 and up.

PULI (Herding)

In their native Hungary *Pulik* (plural of Puli) were used as herders and drovers. They are very active, quick to learn, and make good guard dogs. If the coat is uncombed, it becomes matted and corded much like the coat of the Komondor. Expect moderate to heavy grooming and very little shedding.

coat: Matted, with matting covering head, muzzle, and eyes. *Colors:* solid black, gray, or white.

height/weight: Dog 17″, bitch 16″/approx. 30 lbs.

behavior: A very quick learner, very good with its family, including older children. May be stubborn and self-assured, may be nervous and bark a lot. Needs quite a lot of outdoor exercise.

winning traits: Overall a short-coupled, square animal with a very agile movement and active personality; *head* is slightly domed with a powerful, moderately short muzzle; *ears* are medium-sized, V-shaped, and set somewhat high on the head; *legs* are medium-boned, strong, and parallel; *body* is compact, with a short, strong, loin and a moderately broad, deep chest; *tail* is natural and low-set when relaxed, carried over the back when excited.

disqualify/penalize: More than 1 inch over sizes mentioned above, animals that are very timid.

considerations: May develop hip dysplasia and problems with skin.

price range: $300 and up.

RHODESIAN RIDGEBACK
(Hound)

This breed was developed in South Africa, where they were used to hunt lions. They are used also as guard dogs and watchdogs. They need lots of space to be truly happy, but can stand varied climates and can go without water for a very long time. Expect moderate grooming and shedding.

coat: Short, sleek, shiny, with a ridge of hair along the back which grows toward the front. *Colors:* light to reddish wheaten, small amounts of white on chest and toes permissible.

height/weight: Dog 25"–27"/75 lbs., bitch 24"–26"/65 lbs.

behavior: A quick learner, good with his family and children (if introduced to them at early age), can be aloof with strangers. Stubborn, outgoing, needs firm hand in training. Needs lots of outdoor exercise.

winning traits: Overall a very strong, large animal that gives the impression of great stamina; *head* is wide and flat, medium-long, and has a deep, strong muzzle; *ears* are tapered, medium in size and set high on head; *legs*, front are heavy-boned and straight, hind are very obviously strong and well muscled; *tail* is natural and slightly curved.

disqualify/penalize: Nose that is not black or brown, coat that is woolly, soft, or silky, too much white on chest or stomach.

considerations: Normally healthy but may develop problems with cysts that occur near the hair ridge on back, may be prone to hip dysplasia and cervical deformity

price range: $300 and up.

ROTTWEILER (Working)

In spite of their German-sounding name, they came from ancient Rome. They are excellent guard dogs but were used originally as cattle drovers and for pulling carts; in fact, they often wore their masters' purses around their necks on market day. Expect moderate grooming and shedding.

coat: Flat, short, coarse, with undercoat on neck and thighs. *Colors:* black with tan or mahogany on cheeks, chest, muzzle, legs, and over eyes.

height/weight: Dog 23¾"–27", bitch 21¾"–25¾"/approx. 85 lbs.

behavior: May be a slow learner, very good with his family and children (if raised with them from an early age), may be aloof with strangers. Extremely strong in body and will, can be too aggressive for many, needs early training with a firm hand. Needs lots of outdoor exercise. (This is a breed that is becoming very popular very fast, so be careful in choosing your breeder.)

winning traits: Overall a powerful-looking animal that is both strong and agile; *head* is very broad with a little wrinkling when the dog is alert, and a very muscular broad muzzle; *ears* are somewhat small, wide-set and placed high on head; *legs* are very heavy in muscle and bone and are wide-set, with long powerful thighs, front and back are straight when seen from front or back views; *body* has a straight back, deep chest, and a short, muscular loin; *tail* is docked and normally carried in line with back.

disqualify/penalize: Over or under sizes mentioned above, missing teeth, over/undershot jaw, eyes that do not match, yellow eyes, eyes not identical in shape, coat that is too short, curly, or too long, any color but black as primary color, lack of markings.

considerations: May develop hip dysplasia and digestive problems, may snore.

price range: $500 and up.

SAINT BERNARD (Working)

In keeping with the legend, this lovely giant with his uncanny sense of smell can find people lost in snow. He can also be trained to lie by a lost victim to give warmth until help arrives. There are two varieties (the long-haired and the shorthaired). Expect moderate to heavy grooming and light trimming on the long-haired, light to moderate grooming on the shorthaired. Moderate shedding on both.

SAINT BERNARD: LONG-HAIRED

coat: Shorthaired is thick, smooth, tough, bushy tail; longhaired is medium length on body, shorter on head and ears, curls lightly. *Colors:* white with red, red with white, or brindle with white.

height/weight: Dog, minimum 27½"; bitch, minimum 25½"/121–176½ lbs.

behavior: A quick learner, normal animals love everyone, including lively children. Gentle and mild-mannered. Somewhat inactive indoors, needs lots of outdoor exercise. Recently puppy mills have bred unstable animals; know your breeder before buying

winning traits: Overall a powerful giant with a very intelligent expression; *head* is massive, wide, and has a furrowed and wrinkled brow and short, straight muzzle with ample flews; *ears* are high-set on head and fold so that the outer edge is away from head and inner edge lies close to face; *legs* are extremely strong-boned, powerful, and straight; *body* is very broad and has a moderately deep chest; *tail* is natural and heavy like the rest of the animal, and has a gentle curve.

disqualify/penalize: Too many wrinkles in face, over/undershot jaw, eyelids that are too saggy, eyes that are too red or are too light-colored; tail that is carried over back or is too erect, back that is sway or too long, cowhocks, elbows that bow out.

considerations: May develop hip dysplasia, may be troubled with digestive problems, prone to snoring.

price range: $300–$600.

SAINT BERNARD: SHORT-HAIRED

SALUKI (Hound)

This is the oldest-known pure-bred, domesticated dog in the world. He dates back at least to the time of Alexander the Great (*c.* 329 B.C.) and is known as the Royal Dog of Egypt. He is one of the most elegant dogs and one of the fastest hunters by sight. Expect light grooming and moderate shedding.

coat: Smooth, silky, may be smooth or have feathering on legs and shoulders. *Colors:* red, gold, cream, fawn, grizzle, tan, white, tricolor (white, black, tan), and black and tan.
height/weight: Approx. 23"–28"/60 lbs., bitch normally smaller.
behavior: May be a slow learner, good with his family and older children, may be aloof with strangers and even sometimes with his owner. Well-mannered, stubborn, can be shy. Needs lots of outdoor exercise.
winning traits: Overall an elegant, refined animal that gives the impression of great speed and grace; *head* is long, narrow, and fine; *ears* are long and covered with long, fine hair; *legs*, front are long and straight, hind are long and have low hocks for great speed; *body* has a long, wide back, broad, outstanding hips, and a deep chest; *tail* is long, feathered, and is carried low.
disqualify/penalize: Solid black color.
considerations: None.
price range: $300 and up.

SAMOYED (Working)

This breed is glamorous and dramatic in appearance. For centuries they were herders and guardians of reindeer because of their incredible strength and endurance. In fact, they can run a sled in the bitterest weather for hours before becoming fatigued. Expect moderate to heavy grooming and shedding.

coat: Double coat, undercoat thick, short, soft, outercoat very thick and straight. *Colors:* pure white, white and beige, cream, all beige.

height/weight: Dog 21″–23″, bitch 19″–21″/55 lbs.

behavior: A quick learner, very good with his family, including children, but may be aloof with strangers. Gentle, mild-mannered, can be stubborn and hard to train, may want to roam. Needs lots of outdoor exercise.

winning traits: Overall a very alert animal with balance and proud carriage; *head* is broad and wedge-shaped with a medium-long muzzle that tapers somewhat to the nose; *ears* are thick and erect and well-proportioned to the head; *legs*, front are moderately long, straight, and strong, hind are well bent at the stifles with strong thighs and good movement; *body* has a very deep chest and medium-long straight back, the stomach is well muscled; *tail* is flexible and normally carried over the back, carried down when the animal is relaxed.

disqualify/penalize: Coat color other than those mentioned, blue eye color.

considerations: May develop hip dysplasia.
price range: $300 and up.

SCHIPPERKE (Nonsporting)

This breed's name comes from the Flemish word for little captain, as they were once used as guards on boats. They can be naturally tailless, or tails may be docked. Their foxy head and bright expression make them look fun and mischievous. Expect moderate grooming and trimming.

coat: Thick, harsh, somewhat short on body, dense undercoat, longer and thicker on neck, chest, and back of thighs. *Colors:* solid black.
height/weight: Approx. 12″–13″/under 18 lbs.
behavior: A quick learner, good with and loyal to his adult family, may be aloof with strangers. Can be feisty and quick-tempered. Very active in and out of doors.
winning traits: Overall a highly alert animal with a short-coupled body and a foxy expression; *head* is somewhat wide and foxy with a tapered muzzle; *ears* are very erect and with their high placement add to the overall foxiness of head; *legs* are straight, moderately well boned and muscled; *body* is short and wide with a strong, straight back and a muscular, graceful loin; *tail* is short, either docked or natural.
disqualify/penalize: Dogs that do not hold ears erect, color other than black, over/undershot jaw.

considerations: May be prone to hip dysplasia, eye problems, and dwarfism.
price range: $200–$300.

SCOTTISH DEERHOUND
(Hound)

These are the largest members of the Greyhound family. They are very fast and have tremendous courage, probably making them history's best deerstalkers. In the sixteenth and seventeenth centuries they were the companions of Scottish chieftains. Now in the United States the breed is somewhat rare. Expect to be attentive with grooming, trimming, and stripping. Sheds moderately.

coat: Wiry, hard, 3–4 inches long, rough, lying close to the body, ragged. *Colors:* grays, brindle, yellow, sandy, fawn with black muzzle and ears.
height/weight: Dog 30"–32"/85–110 lbs., bitch approx. 28"/75–95 lbs.
behavior: May be a slow learner, loves everyone, including rough children. Mild-mannered, can be timid and needs patient training. Needs lots of outdoor exercise.
winning traits: Overall a giant animal of great speed and gentle bearing; *head* is long, mustached, narrow at the nose and

widest at the ears; *ears* are dark-colored, small, and high-set on head; *legs*, front are long and wide, hind are on broad hips with well-muscled thighs, with stifles that are quite bent for speed and easy movement; *body* has a deep chest, arched loin, and a back that slopes toward tail from loin; *tail* is natural, long (below hocks), and is carried low.

disqualify/penalize: White facial blaze or white collar, curly or ring tail, woolly coat.

considerations: Normally short-lived, prone to digestive problems, relatively free of hip dysplasia (unusual for a large dog).

price range: $500–$600.

SCOTTISH TERRIER (Terrier)

They are a small and sturdy breed, and have a wonderful sense of themselves. They make excellent apartment companions, as they are independent and can find fun by themselves. In fact, they have such a variety of personalities that owners are seldom bored! They need attentive grooming, stripping, and trimming with a professional hand. Shed little.

coat: Outercoat harsh and wiry, undercoat dense. *Colors:* grays, brindle, grizzle, wheaten, small patch of white permissible on chest.

height/weight: 10"/dog 19–22 lbs., bitch 18–21 lbs.

behavior: A very quick learner, good with his family and somewhat older children, aloof with strangers. May be too active for more sedentary households. Protective, can be stubborn, may bark a lot. Needs some outdoor exercise.

winning traits: Overall a small, compact, powerful animal with bushy eyebrows and short, powerful legs; *head* is long and medium-wide with a slightly rounded skull and a moderately long muzzle; *ears* are very erect, set high on head and naturally pointed; *legs* are very heavy-boned and short, front can be straight or a little bent, hind have very powerful thighs and are straight when seen from behind; *body* has a very deep, wide brisket and short, deep flanks; *tail* is natural but short and carried high.

disqualify/penalize: Coat that is too soft, light-colored eyes,

over/undershot jaw, tail and head not carried erect, shyness.
considerations: Prone to skin, bladder, and kidney problems,
and may develop allergies.
price range: $250 and up.

SEALYHAM TERRIER
(Terrier)

This little fellow has, in a word,
pluck. He is active, brave, and
strong. Originally he was bred
to dig out underground pas-
sages and go after badgers and
other burrowing animals. In
spite of his size, he is very
strong and hardy. The Sealyham coat requires attentive
grooming, stripping, and trimming with a professional hand.
Sheds little.

coat: Undercoat soft and thick, outercoat hard and wiry. *Colors:*
white, white with lemon, tan or beige markings on ears and
head.
height/weight: Approx. 10½"/dog 21 lbs., bitch 20 lbs.
behavior: A quick learner, very good with his family, including
older children, may be aloof with strangers. Can be strong-
willed, normally calmer than most Terriers. Needs moderate
outdoor exercise.
winning traits: Overall a small animal with a rectangular head
and a very powerful build; *head* is very strong, long and wide

with a skull that is lightly domed; *ears* are high-set and round, with the fold level with the top of the head; *legs*, front are very straight and well boned and can be straight or somewhat bent in, hind are a little lighter boned and longer than front; *body* is short and strong, with a back that slants down slightly from the tail to the withers; *tail* is docked and carried straight up.

disqualify/penalize: Over/undershot jaw, flat feet, legs that are not straight, cowhocks, coat that is silky or curly, prick ears or hound ears.

considerations: Prone to skin, back, and eye problems, and may become deaf.

price range: $250–$350.

SHETLAND SHEEPDOG
(Herding)

Agile, fast, and very clever at working a flock of sheep, these dogs are intelligent and are often winners in obedience competition. Both the Shetland Sheepdog and the Collie have a common ancestry in the Scottish Border Collie. They require moderate grooming and some trimming. Expect heavy seasonal shedding.

coat: Outercoat long and straight, undercoat short, furry and thick. *Colors:* black, blue merle, and sable with white or tan markings.

height/weight: 13"–16"/approx. 16 lbs.

behavior: A very quick learner, very intelligent, very good with his family, including children, can be aloof with strangers. Can be shy and nervous but mild-mannered and gentle, may bark a lot. Needs moderate outdoor exercise.

winning traits: Overall a very symmetrical animal with great agility and poise; *head* is long, flat, and has a strong jaw; *ears* are high-set on head, with tips that bend forward when animal is alert; *legs* are straight and strong in both muscle and bone and have strong, wide thighs; *body* is moderately long and has a straight back and deep chest; *tail* is long and full.

disqualify/penalize: Over/undersized animals, coat that is wavy, soft, curly, too silky, animals without undercoat, brindle coloring, rust colors in a black or blue coat, animals that are too shy or nervous or that appear to be bad-tempered, over/

undershot jaw, eyes that are too round or large, ears that are prick or houndlike, tail that is too short or twisted, crooked legs or feet, hackneylike gait.

considerations: May be prone to epilepsy, eye problems, hip dysplasia, and heart problems.

price range: $200 and up.

SHIH TZU (Toy)

These dogs originated in Tibet, and their name means lion in Chinese. The breed is becoming very popular because of its adaptability to apartment living and its bright, merry personality. Some call these dogs "chrysanthemum-faced" for their bright, round expression. Expect to be attentive with grooming. Sheds moderately.

coat: Long, dense, luxurious, can be wavy. *Colors:* any are permissible.

height/weight: 9″–10½″/12–15 lbs.

behavior: A quick learner, likes everyone, including children. Can be stubborn, is active in/outdoors. (Because the breed is becoming very popular, it is best to know your breeder before buying.)

winning traits: Overall a small animal with a proud, upright bearing and a gorgeous coat; *head* is round and wide with a blunt, square, and unwrinkled muzzle and an accentuated stop; *ears* are low-set on head, long, very heavily covered with hair; *legs* are short, strong, well boned and straight with rounded thighs; *body* is strong and moderately long with a wide, deep chest; *tail* is carried high and over back.

disqualify/penalize: Overshot jaw, head that is too narrow, pink nose or rims of eyes, legs that are too long, thin coat, lack of indentation between eyes, light-colored or small eyes.

considerations: May have breathing problems, be bothered by heat, and may develop problems with teeth.

price range: $300 and up.

SIBERIAN HUSKY (Working)

Developed in northeastern Siberia by a nomadic tribe called the Chukchis, this breed pound for pound is considered the toughest draft dog alive. He can pull a loaded sled for miles in the coldest weather and still have energy for more. Even with his heavy coat, this dog has very little odor. Expect moderate grooming and heavy seasonal shedding.

coat: Undercoat dense, soft, outercoat smooth, thick, soft. *Colors:* all colors and markings, face often has a mask.

height/weight: Dog 21"–23½"/45–60 lbs., bitch 20"–22"/35–50 lbs.

behavior: A quick learner, loves everyone, including children. Mild-mannered with all, likes to roam, needs firm, consistent hand in training. Very active indoors and out, needs lots of exercise.

winning traits: Overall an animal that combines stamina, speed, and strength; *head* is medium-sized and somewhat rounded, with a medium-long, straight muzzle; *ears* are medium-sized, erect, thick and set high on head; *legs* are moderately long, heavy-boned, and flexible enough to show great strength, front are straight, hind have well-bent stifles and very muscular thighs; *body* has a deep chest and a medium-long straight back; *tail* is carried high but not tightly to back, may be carried down when dog is relaxed.

disqualify/penalize: Head that is too fine or too heavy, muzzle that is turned up, too short, or too long, ears set too widely or not erect enough, chest that is too broad, ribs too flat, back that is weak, legs that are too heavy or crooked or set too wide, paws that are too big, splayed, or too delicate, tail that is too tightly curled, set too low, or heavily plumed, any gait that is not smooth and effortless, coat that is too long or shaggy, animals over sizes mentioned.

considerations: May be prone to hip dysplasia and cataracts.
price range: $300 and up.

SILKY TERRIER (Toy)

Developed in Australia from crossing the Yorkshire Terrier with the Australian Terrier, these dogs were bred solely as companions and are very good at their job. They have a top-knot from the long, thick hair on their forehead, and need attentive grooming, some skillful trimming. Shed little.

coat: Silky, fine, shiny, 5–6 inches long, parting from head along back to the root of the tail. *Colors:* blue and tan.
height/weight: 9"–10"/8–10 lbs.
behavior: A quick learner, loves everyone. High-spirited, lively, active, can be stubborn, outgoing, may bark a lot. Needs daily exercise.
winning traits: Overall a sprightly animal with a low-set build; *head* is strong, moderately long, and shaped like a wedge; *ears*

are small, erect, and high-set on head; *legs*, front are somewhat fine and straight, hind have strong thighs that are not too heavy; *body* is long and low with a straight back and deep, wide chest; *tail* is docked and set high.

disqualify/penalize: Under/overshot jaw, nails that are white or pink, toes that point in or out.

considerations: None.

price range: $200 and up.

SKYE TERRIER (Terrier)

He was a favorite of Queen Elizabeth I, and by the end of the nineteenth century was the most popular of the Terriers. He is long and low (his length is twice his height), with a beautiful, long coat (5½" or so) that falls over his forehead, protecting the working Skye from injury when hunting. Expect moderate to heavy grooming, and moderate shedding.

coat: Undercoat short, soft, woolly, outercoat long, hard, and straight. *Colors:* black, blue, gray, silver, fawn and cream, black on tips of ears, tail, and muzzle.

height/weight: Dog 10"/bitch 9½"/15½–20 lbs.

behavior: A quick learner, loves his family, good with older children, may be very aloof with strangers if not socialized early. Wants approval very much and is easily trained because of it. Needs moderate outdoor exercise.

winning traits: Overall a small, long, very strong animal with a luxurious coat; *head* is long, strong, and moderately wide; *ears* are either prick and high-set on head or are drop and are close to skull; *legs*, front are short, muscular and straight or slightly bent, hind are muscular and straight when seen from behind; *body* is low to ground, long, and has a deep chest; *tail* is long and carried low when relaxed, straight out as an extension of the back when traveling or excited.

disqualify/penalize: Pink or brown nose.

considerations: None.

price range: $350 and up.

SOFT-COATED WHEATEN
(Terrier)

A multi-use working Terrier, at one time a guard, a cattle dog, and a ratter, he has the liveliness and personality of most Terriers but a lovely soft coat. Originating in Ireland, the breed was officially classified with the American Kennel Club in 1973. Expect heavy to moderate grooming, light trimming and shedding.

coat: Wavy, heavy all over body without an undercoat. *Colors:* all shades of wheaten (puppies may have different coloring until maturity at about two years).

height/weight: Dog 18″–19″/35–40 lbs., bitch 17″–18″/30–35 lbs.

behavior: A quick learner, loves everyone, including active children. Is very active, mild-mannered, gentle, fun-loving. Needs quite a lot of outdoor exercise.

winning traits: Overall medium-sized and angular and has a balanced physique and personality; *head* is rectangular, strong, flat, with a strong muzzle; *ears* are somewhat small, and fold about the top level of the skull, hanging so they point toward ground; *legs* are straight and well boned with strong thighs; *body* has a straight, strong back that is somewhat short with a deep brisket; *tail* is docked and carried high.

disqualify/penalize: Coat that is woolly, harsh, curly, or straight and any color but wheaten, feet turning in or out, animal that is too timid or aggressive, animals that have been trimmed too much, dewclaws on hind legs.

considerations: May suffer from colitis and skin allergies.

price range: $300 and up.

STAFFORDSHIRE BULL TERRIER (Terrier)

A cross between the Bulldog and the progenitor of the Manchester Terrier, this compact, muscular dog was bred to fight other dogs. Long after dog fighting became illegal, the Staffordshire Bull Terrier gained acceptance in the show ring. He is now a fine companion and show dog. Expect light grooming and shedding.

coat: Short, smooth. *Colors:* any colors but black and tan or liver.

height/weight: Dog 14"–16"/28–38 lbs.; bitch 14"–16"/24–34 lbs.

behavior: A quick learner, good with everyone, including children, as long as his family is around. A guard dog by nature and must be kept in control, can be stubborn. Needs moderate outdoor exercise.

winning traits: Overall an animal that is muscular to the extreme with a stable, brave demeanor; *head* is short and has very high, broad cheeks with a wide skull and short forehead;

ears are half-pricked or rose-shaped; *legs* are wide-set and straight when seen from front and back, feet may turn out slightly; *body* is short-coupled with a straight back and wide, deep chest; *tail* is natural and medium-long, with a slight curve that may look like a pump handle.

disqualify/penalize: Pink nose, light-colored eyes, prick ears or ears that drop, curled tail.

considerations: May develop cataracts and tumors.

price range: $300 and up.

STANDARD SCHNAUZER
(Working)

The other two Schnauzer breeds were developed from the Standard Schnauzer. If you seek an all-around dog, give this one a very close look. He is used as a guard dog, a cattle drover, and has been a ratter in the past. He is powerful and has endurance to burn. Expect daily grooming, and a professional hand with stripping and trimming. Sheds little.

coat: Wiry, dense, and tight, undercoat is soft, close to body, outercoat is longer. *Colors:* pure black or salt and pepper.

height/weight: Dog 18½″–19½″, bitch 17½″–18½″/approx. 25 lbs.

behavior: A quick learner, loves and protects his family, good with somewhat grown children. Very loyal, alert, can be stubborn, strong-willed. Very active in and out of doors, needs lots of outdoor exercise.

winning traits: Overall a square, heavyset animal with great energy and a wonderful, free gait; *head* is rectangular and strong, with a straight muzzle that has a line parallel to the head in profile; *ears* are either cropped or uncropped, if cropped they are erect and high-set, when left natural they are small, V-shaped, button ears carried close to head; *legs* are moderately short, very straight, wide-set and parallel when seen from front or back; *body* is short, muscular, agile with a deep chest and a moderately tight, drawn-up stomach; *tail* is docked and erect.

disqualify/penalize: Over/undershot jaw, build that is too slender or bulky, tail carried too far forward, coat that is too smooth, soft, shaggy, or curly, any gait that is not free, confident or powerful, excessive shyness or viciousness, over or under size.

considerations: Normally very healthy but may develop hip dysplasia, prone to tumors.

price range: $300–$450.

SUSSEX SPANIEL (Sporting)

The Sussex Spaniel's tail tells a wonderful story about his cheerful attitude. His breeding makes him a very good, precise but somewhat slow gundog. He is especially good at working in heavy ground cover, which requires strength and agility. The breed is quite rare in the United States. Expect moderate grooming with light trimming, moderate shedding.

coat: Slightly wavy, thick, feathered on legs and tail. *Colors:* rich golden liver

height/weight: 15″–16″/35–45 lbs.

behavior: A somewhat slow learner, loves everyone, including lively children, mild-mannered, kind, may howl a lot. Needs a moderate amount of outdoor exercise.

winning traits: Overall is a low-slung, strong animal that looks strong, methodical and willing to do hard work; *head* is wide and long, somewhat heavy, with a square muzzle that is about 3 inches long and has hanging lips; *ears* are long, somewhat low-set and close to head; *legs* are short, heavy-boned, strong, and have large feet; *body* has a deep chest and a long back; *tail* is carried lower than the line of the back, docked to 5–7 inches and feathered.

disqualify/penalize: Hind legs that are shorter than the front, liver color that is too dark.

considerations: None.

price range: $250–$300.

TIBETAN SPANIEL
(Nonsporting)

The background of these little dogs is as obscure as the area they come from. They were, however, brought to Chinese palaces as gifts from monks, and from there their popularity spread. The first litters outside Tibet were born in England. They became a classified breed with the American Kennel Club in 1984. They are especially popular for a unique personality that has been compared to that of a cat. Expect light grooming and shedding.

coat: Natural (needs no trimming), double, moderately long and flat on the body, short on the face, and feathered on the tail and rump. *Colors:* all are permissible.

height/weight: Approx. 10"/9–15 lbs.

behavior: A quick learner, gentle, mild-mannered. Does not need much outdoor exercise.

winning traits: Overall a small animal with a body that is somewhat long, with a plumed tail that balances the head; *head* is small and has a medium-long muzzle with a deep, wide chin; *ears* are high-set, hanging, and with a fold beginning a little higher than the skull; *legs,* front are mildly bowed with moderate bone, hind are strong and straight when seen from behind; *body* is somewhat long and deep, with a straight back; *tail* is high-set, plumed, and held over back.

disqualify/penalize: Nervousness, acutely bowed front legs, feet that are catlike, over/undershot jaw, large bulging eyes, light-colored eyes, skull that is too domed, flat, or wide.
considerations: May be bothered by hot weather.
price range: $250 and up.

TIBETAN TERRIER
(Nonsporting)

This breed is almost two thousand years old and comes from a very remote region of Tibet, where it is given as a symbol of luck to visitors. They are hardy enough to withstand the vigorous winters of their native country, but in spite of their name, they are not truly Terriers and have not the Terrier personality. Expect moderate grooming and shedding.

coat: Double, undercoat is woolly and fine, outercoat is thick, long, and either straight or wavy. *Colors:* any are permissible.
height/weight: 14″–16″/18–30 lbs.
behavior: May be a slow learner, loves his family but is aloof with strangers, may be timid. Needs moderate outdoor exercise.
winning traits: Overall a squarish animal with lots of hair and

a lovely, intelligent personality; *head* is medium-long and flat; *ears* are hanging, V-shaped, and covered with heavy feathering; *legs* are straight from front and back views; *body* is short-coupled and very strong; *tail* is natural, plumed, and is carried high over back.

disqualify/penalize: Nose that is not black, under/overshot jaw, snipy face.

considerations: May have skin problems and eye disorders.

price range: $300 and up.

VIZSLA (Sporting)

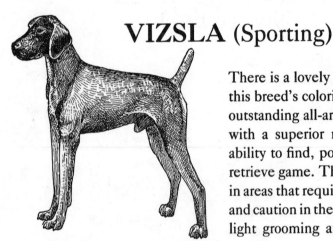

There is a lovely uniformity to this breed's coloring. They are outstanding all-around hunters with a superior nose and the ability to find, point, and then retrieve game. They work best in areas that require both speed and caution in the hunt. Expect light grooming and shedding.

coat: Short, smooth, thick. *Colors:* rust-gold, sandy with the darker shades preferred, a few white hairs on toes and chest permissible.

height/weight: Dog 22″–24″, bitch 21″–23″/approx. 65 lbs.

behavior: A quick learner, loves everyone, including children. Obeys readily, mild-mannered, normally easygoing. Needs lots of outdoor exercise. (Popularity is rising and puppy mills are beginning to breed timid animals; know your breeder.)

winning traits: Overall an elegant, medium-sized animal with strength and stamina; *head* is lean, strong, and has a straight, strong muzzle; *ears* hang close to head, are somewhat long and rounded at ends; *legs*, front are straight with catlike feet, hind are straight from behind with moderately angulated stifles; *tail* is docked but left somewhat long.

disqualify/penalize: Undocked tail, middle toes much longer than rest of digits, black color in coat, animals over or under size by more than 1½ inches, black nose, large amount of white on chest, white anywhere on body of animal.

considerations: Normally healthy but may be prone to skin and blood disorders and epilepsy.

price range: $300 and up.

WEIMARANER (Sporting)

This breed originated in Germany. Here in the United States they have been referred to as the "Gray Ghost" because of their coloring and their excellent speed and heart. They are also known for their superior nose, and are some of the best hunting dogs for either land or water. They also excel in obedience competition. Expect light to moderate grooming and light shedding.

coat: Smooth, short, tight. *Colors:* solid shades of gray, usually a little lighter on head, small white mark on chest permissible.
height/weight: Dog 25"–27"/65–85 lbs., bitch 23"–25"/55–75 lbs.
behavior: A quick learner, good with his family, including older children, but may be aloof with strangers. Very active, strong-willed, very lively. Needs lots of outdoor exercise.
winning traits: Overall a sleek, graceful animal built for speed and strength; *head* is moderately long with a clean, tight muzzle; *ears* are high-set, long, and lightly folded; *legs* are strong and straight in front, hind are well-muscled and straight from behind with well-bent stifles; *body* is moderately long with a straight back and a slight slope to the tail, and loins that are moderately tucked up; *tail* is docked about 6 inches long.
disqualify/penalize: Over or under size by more than 1 inch, too long a coat, coat that is blue or black, tail that is too long or short, pink-colored nose, animal that is not in top physical

condition, four or more teeth missing, poor movement, legs and feet that are not straight and strong, back that is not straight, over/undershot jaw, white anywhere but as a small spot on chest, eyes that are any color but gray, blue-gray, or amber, skittish animals.

considerations: Prone to digestive problems, hip dysplasia, and problems with gait.

price range: $300–$400.

WELSH CORGI-CARDIGAN
(Herding)

Corgi is the word for dog in Celtic. The ancestors of this breed were known in Wales for three thousand years. They are heeling cattle drovers and, in spite of their short legs, are fast and powerful. The Cardigan is the rarest of the Corgis in the United States. Expect moderate grooming and shedding.

coat: Double, thick, medium in length. *Colors:* red, brindle, tricolor, black, sable, blue merle, usually with white markings.

height/weight: Approx. 12″/20 lbs.

behavior: A very quick learner, loves his family, including children, may be aloof with strangers. Very devoted and loyal, protective, obeys readily, extremely alert. Active in and outdoors, needs moderate outdoor exercise but is well suited to apartment life.

winning traits: Overall a low, long dog with a mild, intelligent manner; *head* is somewhat wide across the skull and has a moderately short muzzle with strong jaws; *ears* are erect, large and rounded; *legs*, front are very short and well boned with a mild curve at the wrists; hind are very strong; *body* is muscular and strong with a deep chest and a short, firm loin; *tail* is short, set low.

disqualify/penalize: Over/undershot jaw, ears that drop or hang, nose color other than black (except in merles), ears that are too small or too pointed, tail carried too high, splayed toes, long or fluffy coat, blue eyes, any coat color but those mentioned above or color that is mostly white.

considerations: Subject to back problems.

price range: $250 and up.

WELSH CORGI-PEMBROKE
(Herding)

Though this breed's appearance is similar to that of the
Cardigan Corgi, it is from different ancestry. Like the Cardigan, he is a cattle dog,
nipping at the heels of cattle to
herd them. Though the tail is
normally docked, some animals
are born tailless. Expect moderate grooming and shedding.

coat: Double with outer coat that is thick, medium length.
Colors: red, sable, fawn, black, tan with and without white
markings.

height/weight: 10″–12″/dog 20–24 lbs., bitch 18–22 lbs.

behavior: A very quick learner, likes everyone, including
children. Mild-mannered, somewhat more outgoing and excitable than the Cardigan, obeys readily. Very active, needs
moderate outdoor exercise.

winning traits: Overall a long, low dog with an alert, intelligent expression; *head* is wide, flat, and foxy with a straight
muzzle; *ears* are erect, medium-sized, and rounded at tips; *legs*
are short, turning in somewhat at the wrists and are well boned,
hind have muscular thighs, with movement that is smooth and
agile in spite of the short legs; *body* has a deep chest, hips a little
narrower than the shoulders, a straight back (slight indentation
behind the shoulders is permissible); *tail* is docked and very
short.

disqualify/penalize: Shyness or viciousness, over or under-
sized animals, over/undershot jaw, button ears or ears that drop,

neck too short or too long, double-jointed hocks, feet too long, short, narrow or round, black with white but no tan color, predominantly white color with red or dark markings, whole-colored dogs with white between withers and tail, a bluish tint to coat or white on sides between elbows and hindquarters or white on ears, coat that is too long and feathered heavily.
considerations: May develop back problems.
price range: $300 and up.

WELSH SPRINGER SPANIEL (Sporting)

This beautiful breed is found in almost every country of the world. He is not only an excellent hunter but can stand intense heat and bitter cold. He is an instinctive hunter but unless trained early will develop habits that are hard to break later on. Expect moderate grooming and some fairly difficult trimming. Sheds moderately.

coat: Thick, straight, silky. *Colors:* rich red and white.
height/weight: 15″–16″/35–45 lbs.
behavior: A quick learner, is very good with his family, including children, may be reserved with strangers. Loving in a quiet way, mild-mannered. Needs lots of outdoor exercise.
winning traits: Overall a compact animal of enduring strength and stamina, with a cheerful disposition; *head* is medium-long and has a slight dome; *ears* are low-set, somewhat small, feathered, and hang close to head; *legs,* front are medium-long and

straight with good bone, hind are medium-long and have a moderate bend to stifle; *body* has a deep chest and is strong with a strong loin; *tail* is docked.

disqualify/penalize: Head that is short and stocky.

considerations: Prone to epilepsy, and can be troubled with ear infections.

price range: $150–$250.

WELSH TERRIER (Terrier)

Welsh Terriers were bred in Wales for hunting badgers, foxes, and otters, and they have great strength and intelligence. They have at times been called Old English Terriers or Black and Tan Wirehaired Terriers. They are very lively, and though small they have the spirit of a larger dog. Need attentive grooming, trimming, and stripping with a professional hand. Shed little.

coat: Wiry, thick, hard. *Colors:* black or black grizzle and tan.

height/weight: Dog 15″, bitch 14″/approx. 20 lbs.

behavior: A quick learner, lots of life, loves everyone including children. Very hardy smaller dog, active in and out of doors. Needs moderate outdoor exercise.

winning traits: Overall an animal with a compact, angular profile and a friendly, outgoing posture; *head* is rectangular, very strong, has a flat skull and strong, square muzzle; *ears* are small, carried so they fold just above the top of the skull and tend forward toward the eyes; *legs*, front are strong and straight; hind have muscular thighs and small feet; *body* has a straight back, deep, wide chest, and a strong loin; *tail* is docked and carried high.

disqualify/penalize: Aggressive or overly timid behavior.

considerations: Normally healthy but may be bothered by dry skin, allergies, and eye problems.

price range: $300 and up.

WEST HIGHLAND WHITE TERRIER (Terrier)

Even though small, these little fellows are spunky watchdogs. They are also showy performers. Their ears are naturally stiffly erect and uncropped and seem to act as a counterbalance for their upright tails. Expect somewhat attentive grooming, trimming, and stripping, but little shedding.

coat: Outercoat about 2″ long, double, straight, undercoat soft and furry. *Colors:* white.

height/weight: Dog 11″, bitch 10″/16 lbs.

behavior: A quick learner, likes everyone, including older children. Very lively and active, can be strong-willed, as most Terriers can, but is normally easily trained. Needs moderate outdoor exercise.

winning traits: Overall a short, neat, and compact animal with a short, wide head and smart, sassy demeanor; *head* is wide, short, powerful, and has a muzzle that is shorter than the skull; *ears* are almost rigidly erect, very pointed, wide-set, and should be trimmed so there is no fringe; *legs* are short and strong, front are straight or slightly bent, hind are very strong with muscular thighs; *body* has a straight back, is compact and wide with strong hips; *tail* is natural, short and carried high.

disqualify/penalize: Coat any color but white, coat that curls or is silky, head that is too long or narrow, under/overshot jaw, ears that are not small, compact, and erect, long or weak back, crooked or cowhock legs, tail that is too long, carried over back, or too low, stiff movement, excessive shyness or aggressiveness.

considerations: Normally healthy but may be bothered by skin problems, allergies, and deficiency with tearing.

price range: $300–$400.

WHIPPET (Hound)

This breed was developed by crossing small Greyhounds with Terriers, but the Terrier ancestry is hardly noticeable. They are able to race where space is limited, often being clocked at 35 miles an hour. In the United States they have become popular house pets and are clean enough for those who are normally bothered by allergies. Expect minimal grooming, little shedding.

coat: Short, firm, close. *Colors:* any are permissible.

height/weight: Dog 19″–22″, bitch 18″–21″/approx. 10–28 lbs.

behavior: A quick learner, likes an adult family, may be aloof with strangers. Easily trained if trained with a soft, gentle touch, may be timid, but is more outgoing than he looks. Needs lots of outdoor exercise.

winning traits: Overall an animal with a slight and refined outline, giving the impression of speed even when not moving; *head* is narrow and long with a long, strong muzzle; *ears* are small and folded to lay pointing back when dog is relaxed, semi-prick when dog is alert; *legs*, front are long, well boned and well muscled, hind are very long and strong with wide hips; *body* has back that is wide and gracefully arched, a very deep, strong chest; *tail* is natural, set low and slightly curved.

disqualify/penalize: Blue eyes, undershot jaw or uneven bite, more than ½ inch above or below sizes mentioned above, any movement that is restricted or not free, legs crossing in front of each other, ears that are erect, tail that curls, short loin, flat croup.

considerations: May be bothered by cold, very sensitive to drugs, may not develop fully descended testicles.

price range: $200 and up.

WIREHAIRED POINTING GRIFFON (Sporting)

This breed was developed in Holland for hunting and retrieving pheasants and water birds. It traveled to France, where it became quite popular, but it is fairly rare in the United States. An excellent swimmer with a rough, protective coat, it is particularly good in swampy areas. Expect moderate grooming, trimming, and stripping.

coat: Outercoat stiff and hard, with a downy undercoat. *Colors:* gray, or gray and white with chestnut flecks, chestnut or dirty white mixed with chestnut.

height/weight: Dog 21½″–23½″, bitch 19½″—21½″.

behavior: A quick learner, loves his family and children, may be aloof with strangers. Mild-mannered, can be skittish in noisy surroundings, not suited for cities. Very active indoors and out, needs lots of outdoor exercise.

winning traits: Overall an animal with vigorous strength and a bristled appearance; *head* is long, with eyebrows and a bristled, square muzzle; *ears* are high-set, medium-sized, and lie flat, with little hair; *legs* are straight when viewed from front or back, and are long and strong; *body* has a straight, strong back; *tail* is docked to about one-third its natural length.

disqualify/penalize: Curly coat, black color, any color nose but brown.

considerations: May develop hip dysplasia.

price range: $250–$300.

YORKSHIRE TERRIER (Toy)

This is the most popular Toy breed in England. The puppies are black at birth and change to adult colors later. When first developed, the breed was much larger and was used to kill rodents. They are now simply among the best house pets for those who do not mind attentive grooming. Expect little shedding.

coat: Long, silky, fine, shiny. *Colors:* body dark steel blue, head and legs tan, chest bright tan.

height/weight: 8″–9″/not over 7 lbs.

behavior: A quick learner, likes everyone, including older children. May bark a lot, very active in and out of doors. Needs little outdoor exercise.

winning traits: Overall a tiny animal that is low-set and compact, with a luxurious coat; *head* is small but well proportioned and somewhat flat, with a muzzle of moderate proportion; *ears* are V-shaped, somewhat small, and carried erect; *legs* are straight when seen from front or back; *body* is compact and has a moderately short, straight back; *tail* is docked and carried high.

disqualify/penalize: Weight over 7 pounds, black hair intermingled with tan, ears too far apart.

considerations: May develop slipped stifle, epilepsy, eye problems, when giving birth bitch may develop calcium imbalance.

price range: $300–$400.

GLOSSARY OF TERMS

APPLE HEAD: A head (skull) that is very rounded or bulbous.

BACK: The top line of the animal.

BAT EARS: Ears that are broad at the base, erect, rounded at the top, and directed toward the front.

BITCH: The female dog.

BRINDLE: A mixture of light and dark colors with black.

BRISKET: The part of the chest that is between the front legs, may be used interchangeably with the word chest in the text.

BUTTON EARS: Ears in which the soft flap folds forward and down toward the eyes.

CHEST: The part of the dog that encases the ribs, heart, lungs.

CHERRY NOSE: A pink-colored nose that is faulted in particular breeds.

CLEAN MUZZLE: A muzzle without excess or hanging skin.

CLIPPED EARS: Ears that have been surgically cut to shape according to certain breed standards.

COBBY BUILD: A build that is short-coupled and muscular.

COMPACT BUILD: Short-coupled build.

COWHOCKS: Back leg joints (hocks) that bend in toward each other.

CROUP: The part of the dog's back that is over its hind legs and before the tail.

DEWCLAWS: A useless fifth toe found inside the leg and above the foot.

DEWLAP: Loose hanging skin under the throat.

DOCKED TAIL: A tail that has been shortened by cutting.

DOME: The rounded part of the skull.

DOG: The male dog. Also used collectively to indicate either the male or the female.

DOUBLE COAT: A coat that has two types of hairs: the outer hairs that protect against brambles and weather, the inner hairs that are softer and protect against weather and water.

DROP EARS: Soft, pendulous ears hanging close to the head.

DUDLEY NOSE: A pink or flesh-colored nose.

ELBOWS: The joints at the top of the front legs just above the forearms.

FALLOW COLORING: Light cream color, light yellow, and light yellow-red.

FEATHERING: Fringes of long hair.

FETLOCK: The joint on the hind leg, above the foot.

FLEWS: Hanging inner corners of the upper lips.

GRIZZLE (COLOR): Blue-gray.

HACKNEY GAIT: A high-stepping movement of the front legs.

HARLEQUIN: Patches of color on a solid background of color. Usually black on white.

HEIGHT: The measurement from the ground to the withers.

HIP DYSPLASIA: A malformation of the hip that can lead to pain and arthritis.

HOCK: The protruding joint in the hind leg that corresponds to the heel in humans.

HOUND'S EARS: Ears that are low-set and long like those of the Hound.

LOIN: Section of the topline between last rib and hips.

MERLE: Blue-gray coloring with black flecks.

MUZZLE: The part of the head that is before the eyes.

NOSE: The part of the dog used for smelling, situated at the point of the muzzle.

OFA CERTIFIED: Certification from the Orthopedic Foundation for Animals that an animal is free of hip dysplasia.

OVERSHOT JAW: A jaw that has the top teeth overlapping the bottom teeth.

PARTI-COLORED: A coat of two or more colors that are about equal in proportion.

PIEBALD: Covered with patches or spots of two colors.

PRICK EARS: Sharp, pointed ears that are carried erect.

RAT TAIL: A tail that is thick at the root and tapers to a point and is bare of hair at the end.

ROACH BACK: A back that curves higher toward the loin.

ROAN COLORING: Colors that are finely mixed in the coat.

ROMAN NOSE: A nose with a bridge that is convex.

RUFF: Long, thick mane on the neck of some animals.

SHORT-COUPLED: Short in body from forequarters to hindquarters.

SNIPY MUZZLE: A muzzle that is pointed, narrow, and weak.

SQUARE BUILD: A build that forms a square when measured from shoulder to upper thigh and from the ground to the point of the shoulder.

STRIPPING: Pulling or plucking dead hairs from the coat (especially in the wirehaired breeds).

STIFLE: The thigh joint in the hind legs, compares to the human knee.

STOP: The step up from the muzzle to the skull.

TICKED COLORING: Coloring that has small splashes of darker color on a white background.

TOPKNOT: A patch of hair on top of the head.

TOPLINE: The upper line of the back, along the spine.

TRIMMING: Grooming by clipping or plucking.

TUCK-UP: The part of the underline that rises just behind the ribs and under the loin.

UNDERSHOT JAW: A jaw that has the lower teeth protruding from under the upper teeth.

WALL EYES: Eyes that turn outward, showing a greater-than-normal amount of white.

WHEATEN COLOR: Fawn or light yellow.

WITHERS: The top part of the shoulders just behind the neck.

BIBLIOGRAPHY

American Kennel Club. *The Complete Dog Book*. New York: Howell Book House, 1987.

Ashworth, Lou Sawyer. *The Dell Encyclopedia of Dogs*. New York: Delacorte Press, 1974.

Barnes, Duncan, and Staff of the American Kennel Club. *The AKC's World of the Pure Bred Dog*. New York: Howell Book House, 1983.

Bartos, Bob. *The Dog for You*. New York: Dell Publishing, 1974.

Bongianni, Maurizio, and Concetta Mori. *Dogs of the World*. New York: Crescent Books, 1988.

Caras, Roger. *Harper's Illustrated Handbook of Dogs*. New York: Harper & Row, 1987.

Dog Fancy. Irvine, CA: Fancy Publications, Inc.

Howe, John. *Choosing the Right Dog*. New York: Harper & Row, 1980.

Pure-bred Dogs/American Kennel Gazette. New York: The American Kennel Club, Inc.

Schuler, Elizabeth Meriwether. *Simon and Schuster's Guide to Dogs*. New York: Simon & Schuster, 1980.

Tortora, Daniel F. *The Right Dog for You*. New York: Simon & Schuster, 1983

World Almanac and Book of Facts 1989. New York: Pharos Books, 1989.